IMPACT

CALIFORNIA SOCIAL STUDIES

Continuity and Change

INQUIRY JOURNAL

Mc
Graw
Hill
Education

Program Authors

James Banks, Ph.D.
Kerry and Linda Killinger Endowed Chair
in Diversity Studies
Director, Center for Multicultural Education
University of Washington
Seattle, Washington

Kevin P. Colleary, Ed.D.
Curriculum and Teaching Department
Graduate School of Education
Fordham University
New York, New York

William Deverell, Ph.D.
Director of the Huntington-USC Institute
on California and the West
Professor of History, University
of Southern California
Los Angeles, California

Daniel Lewis, Ph.D.
Dibner Senior Curator
The Huntington Library
Los Angeles, California

Elizabeth Logan Ph.D., J.D.
Associate Director of the Huntington-
USC Institute on California and the West
Los Angeles, California

Walter C. Parker, Ph.D.
Professor of Social Studies Education
Adjunct Professor of Political Science
University of Washington
Seattle, Washington

Emily M. Schell, Ed.D.
Professor, Teacher Education
San Diego State University
San Diego, California

mheducation.com/prek-12

Copyright © 2019 McGraw-Hill Education

Send all inquiries to:
McGraw-Hill Education
303 East Wacker Drive, Suite 2000
Chicago, IL 60601

ISBN: 978-0-07-899393-0
MHID: 0-07-899393-8

Printed in the United States of America.

4 5 6 7 8 9 QSX 22 21 20 19 18

Letter from the Authors

Dear Social Studies Detective,

Why did people settle in California? Who were the first people who lived in your community—and why did they choose to live there? In this book, you will find out more about communities. You will think about the issues important in your community and what **you** can do to help!

As you read, be an investigator. What do you wonder about? Write your own questions and read closely to find the answers. What in this book interests you? What do you find exciting? Take notes about it and analyze your notes. Then you can use your notes to do a project to share what you've learned. Take a closer look at photos of real people and places. Use maps and timelines to think about how California and your community have changed.

Enjoy your investigation into the amazing world of social studies—a place where people live in communities that grow and change, a place where **you** can make a difference!

Sincerely,

The IMPACT Social Studies Authors

San Francisco Bay Bridge in the 1940s

Contents

Reference Sources

Communities in California

 How Does Geography Impact California Communities?

Chapter 2

American Indians of the Local Region

 ESSENTIAL EQ QUESTION **How Have California Indians Influenced the Local Region?**

Chapter 3

How and Why Communities Change Over Time

How Has Life Changed for People in My Community Over Time?

Chapter 4

American Citizens, Symbols, and Government

 How Do Our Government and Its Citizens Work Together?

Economics of the Local Region

 How Do People in a Community Meet Their Needs?

Skills and Features

Inquiry and Analysis Skills

Reader's Theater

Getting Started

You have two social studies books that you will use together to explore and analyze important Social Studies issues.

The Inquiry Journal

The Inquiry Journal is your reporter's notebook where you will ask questions, analyze sources, and record information.

The Research Companion

The Research Companion is where you'll read nonfiction and literature selections, examine primary source materials, and look for answers to your questions.

Every Chapter

Chapter opener pages help you see the big picture. Each chapter begins with an **Essential Question**. This **EQ** guides research and inquiry.

In the **Research Companion**, you'll explore the EQ through words and photographs.

In the **Inquiry Journal**, you'll talk about the EQ and find out about the EQ Inquiry Project for the chapter.

StasKhom/iStock/Getty Images

Explore Words

Find out what you know about the chapter's academic vocabulary.

Connect Through Literature

Explore the chapter topic through fiction, informational text, and poetry.

Connect Through Literature

Visions of URBAN CALIFORNIA
by Harvey Jones

California's early painters liked to paint landscapes showing the state's spectacular natural beauty. In the 1800s, many settlers came to California. They were attracted by this beauty, and by the promise of gold, rich farmland, or a new life. Cities sprang up, and urban growth changed California's landscape forever. California artists have painted the urban landscape in many ways. They show its excitement, its harsh realities, its promise, and its human-made beauty.

William Hahn's *Sacramento Railroad Station* shows a busy railroad station in 1870s Sacramento. Hahn was a master of a type of painting called "genre." Genre paintings show people doing everyday things. These paintings reveal something about life in a particular time and place. They are similar to today's candid (unposed) photographs. In this genre painting, Hahn is not trying to present a beautiful and flattering view of Sacramento. He wants to show city life as realistically as possible.

California Pines, painted by William Keith in 1878

Sacramento Railroad Station, painted by William Hahn in 1874

110 Chapter 3 How and Why Communities Change Over Time

Chapter 3 111

People You Should Know

Learn about the lives of people who have made an impact in history.

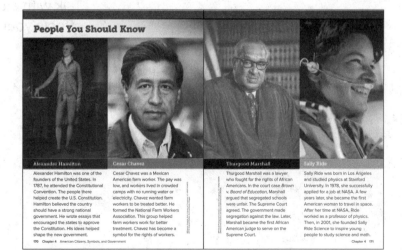

People You Should Know

Alexander Hamilton

Alexander Hamilton was one of the founders of the United States. In 1787, he attended the Constitutional Convention. The people there helped create the U.S. Constitution. Hamilton believed the country should have a strong national government. He wrote essays that encouraged the states to approve the Constitution. His ideas helped shape the new government.

Cesar Chavez

Cesar Chavez was a Mexican American farm worker. The pay was low, and workers lived in crowded camps with no running water or electricity. Chavez wanted farm workers to be treated better. He formed the National Farm Workers Association. This group helped farm workers work for better treatment. Chavez has become a symbol for the rights of workers.

Thurgood Marshall

Thurgood Marshall was a lawyer who fought for the rights of African Americans. In the court case *Brown v. Board of Education*, Marshall argued that segregated schools were unfair. The Supreme Court agreed. The government made segregation against the law. Later, Marshall became the first African American judge to serve on the Supreme Court.

Sally Ride

Sally Ride was born in Los Angeles and studied physics at Stanford University. In 1978, she successfully applied for a job at NASA. A few years later, she became the first American woman to travel in space. After her time at NASA, Ride worked as a professor of physics. Then, in 2001, she founded Sally Ride Science to inspire young people to study science and math.

170 Chapter 4 American Citizens, Symbols, and Government

Chapter 4 171

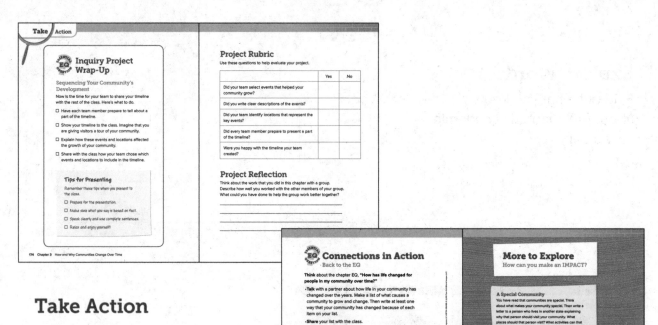

Take Action

Present your Inquiry Project to your class and assess your work with the project rubric. Then take time to reflect on your work.

Connections in Action

Think about the people, places, and events you read about in the chapter. Talk with a partner about how this affects your understanding of the EQ.

Every Lesson

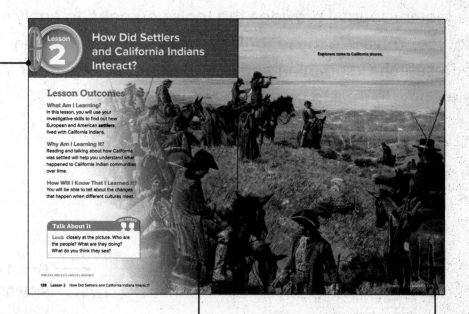

Lesson Question lets you think about how the lesson connects to the chapter EQ.

Lesson Outcomes help you think about what you will be learning and how it applies to the EQ.

Images and text provide opportunities to explore the lesson topic.

Lesson selections help you develop a deeper understanding of the lesson topic and the EQ.

Analyze and Inquire

The Inquiry Journal provides the tools you need to analyze a source. You'll use those tools to investigate the texts in the Research Companion and use the graphic organizer in the Inquiry Journal to organize your findings.

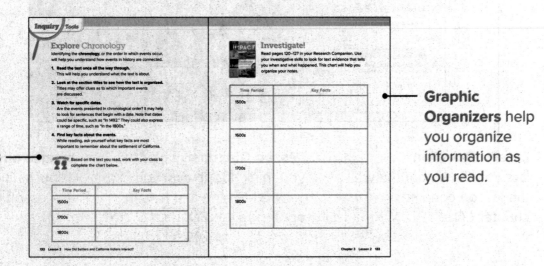

Inquiry Tools assist with analysis and exploration.

Graphic Organizers help you organize information as you read.

Primary Sources let you read the words and study the artifacts of people from the past and present.

Maps show where events happened.

Stop and Check boxes provide opportunities to check your understanding, consider different perspectives and make connections.

Report Your Findings

At the end of each lesson you have an opportunity in the Inquiry Journal to report your findings and connect back to the EQ. In the Research Companion, you'll think about the lesson focus question.

Report Your Findings

Think About It
Gather Evidence
Review your research. Based on the information you have gathered, how did the lives of California Indians change with the arrival of newcomers?

Write About It
Write and Cite Evidence
In your opinion, what are some positive things that happen when different cultures meet? What are some negative things?

Talk About It
Defend Your Claim
Take turns discussing your responses with a classmate. Do you think the meeting of cultures in early California was more positive or negative?

Connect to the EQ
Pull It Together
Think about the people and events that you read and talked about in this lesson. How did they change things for California today?

Inquiry Project Notes

134 Lesson 2 How Did Settlers and California Indians Interact?

Chapter 3 Lesson 2 135

Think about what you have learned.

Write about it using text evidence to support your ideas.

Connect to the EQ.

Grapes growing in California

Physical Geography of California Communities

California's physical geography has played an important role in the state's history. People settled in places because of the land, water, and climate there. The geography continues to impact why people come to the state and where they live.

Many settlers came to California because of its fertile soil. The flat, rich land in the Central Valley was perfect for farming. As more farmers settled here, towns formed. Farmers sold their goods in places such as Sacramento and Fresno. Both cities had railroads. These allowed farmers to ship their goods around the country. Today, most of our nation's fruit, nuts, and vegetables come from this region. The fertile soil in Napa Valley also brought settlers to California. This valley region is known for growing many crops such as grapes, olives, peaches, pears, and walnuts.

In the mid-1800s, gold was discovered in California's mountains. Miners from all over the world came here. They hoped to get rich quickly. Small communities were built around these mines. When the mountains ran out of gold and silver, people moved away from the communities they had built. These empty towns were called "ghost towns." Today, tourists visit old mining communities to learn about the past.

California's coastal region also became a popular location for people to live. Areas with busy shipping ports often developed into large cities. This is because they were perfect locations for trade. The shipping industry moves goods to and from California. People also chose to live along the coast because of the warm climate and the beautiful beaches. The people who live in San Diego, Santa Monica, and Malibu enjoy both the surf and sun.

✓ Stop and Check

Think How did the physical geography of California influence the growth of communities?

Container ship at the port of Long Beach

What Do You Think? How are communities in California today similar to and different from communities in the past?

136 Lesson 3 How Do Communities of the Past Compare to Today?

Chapter 4 Lesson 3 137

Think about what you read in the lesson. How does this give you a new understanding about the lesson focus question?

Be a Social Studies Detective

How do you learn about people, places, and events?
Become a Social Studies Detective!

Explore!   Investigate!   Report!

Investigate Primary Sources

Detectives solve mysteries by asking questions and searching for clues to help them answer their questions. Where can you get clues that will help you learn about the past? By analyzing primary and secondary sources!

What are Primary Sources?

A **primary source** is a record of an event by someone who was present at whatever he or she is describing. **What are some primary sources?** Clothing, photographs, toys, tools, letters, diaries, and bank records are all examples of primary sources.

Did You Know?

A **secondary source** is information from someone who was not present at the event he or she is describing. Secondary sources are based on primary sources, such as a newspaper article.

A classroom long ago

Social Studies Detective Strategies

Inspect

- Look closely at the source.
- Who or what is it?
- How would you describe it?

Find Evidence

- Where did the event take place?
- When did it happen?
- What are the most important details?

Make Connections

- Is this source like others you found?
- Are there other perspectives that you need to consider?
- What information supports your idea?

Social Studies Detectives make connections to learn about the past. Look closely at the image below. Use the Social Studies Detective Strategy to analyze the image.

Social Studies Detective Strategies

1. Inspect
2. Find Evidence
3. Make Connections

Talk About It

COLLABORATE

After you look closely and ask questions about the image and find evidence to support your ideas. Look for evidence, or details in the picture that support your ideas. Share your evidence and make connections to what you know.

Here is another source. Inspect the source, and look for clues to answer your questions and make connections.

NO PLACE LIKE SAGAMORE HILL

(To Ethel, at Sagamore Hill)
White House, June 11, 1906.

BLESSED ETHEL:

I am very glad that what changes have been made in the house are good, and I look forward so eagerly to seeing them. After all, fond as I am of the White House and much though I have appreciated these years in it, there isn't any place in the world like home—like Sagamore Hill, where things are our own, with our own associations, and where it is real country.

MORE ABOUT QUENTIN

White House, Nov. 22, 1908.

DEAREST ARCHIE:

I handed your note and the two dollar bill to Quentin, and he was perfectly delighted. It came in very handy, because poor Quentin has been in bed with his leg in a plaster cast, and the two dollars I think went to make up a fund with which he purchased a fascinating little steam-engine, which has been a great source of amusement to him. He is out to-day visiting some friends, although his leg is still in a cast. He has a great turn for mechanics.

from *Theodore Roosevelt's Letters to His Children*

Roosevelt, Theodore, Theodore Roosevelt's Letters To His Children, Edited by Joseph Bucklin Bishop. New York, NY: Charles Scribner's Sons, 1919.

Explore Geography

Geographers are social studies detectives who study the Earth's surface, plants, animals, and people. They use tools to help them investigate. Here are a few of the tools you need to be a geographer.

StasKhom/iStock/Getty Images

Reading a Map

A map is a drawing of a place. This map shows the United States. Most maps have features that help us use them.

Map Title The map title names the areas shown on the map. The title may also tell you the kind of information shown on the map, such as roads or landforms.

Inset Map An inset map is a small map included on a larger map. The inset map might show an area that is too large, too small, or too far away to be included on the main map.

Boundary Lines Boundary lines show divisions between states and countries. The boundaries between states usually are drawn differently from the boundaries between nations.

Locator Map A locator map is a small map on a larger map. It shows the area of the map in a larger region.

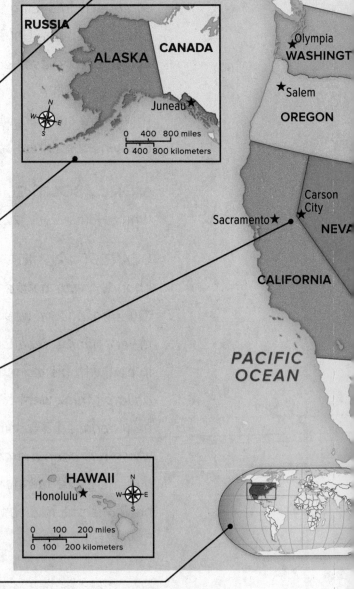

The United States of America

RUSSIA
CANADA
ALASKA
Juneau
N W E S
0 400 800 miles
0 400 800 kilometers

Olympia
WASHINGT
Salem
OREGON

Carson City
Sacramento
NEVA
CALIFORNIA

PACIFIC OCEAN

HAWAII
Honolulu
N W E S
0 100 200 miles
0 100 200 kilometers

Scale Distances on Earth are too far to show on a map. To figure out the real distance between two places on a map, you use the scale. The scale shows the relationship between distances on a map and real distances.

Compass Rose The compass rose shows where north, south, east, and west are on the map.

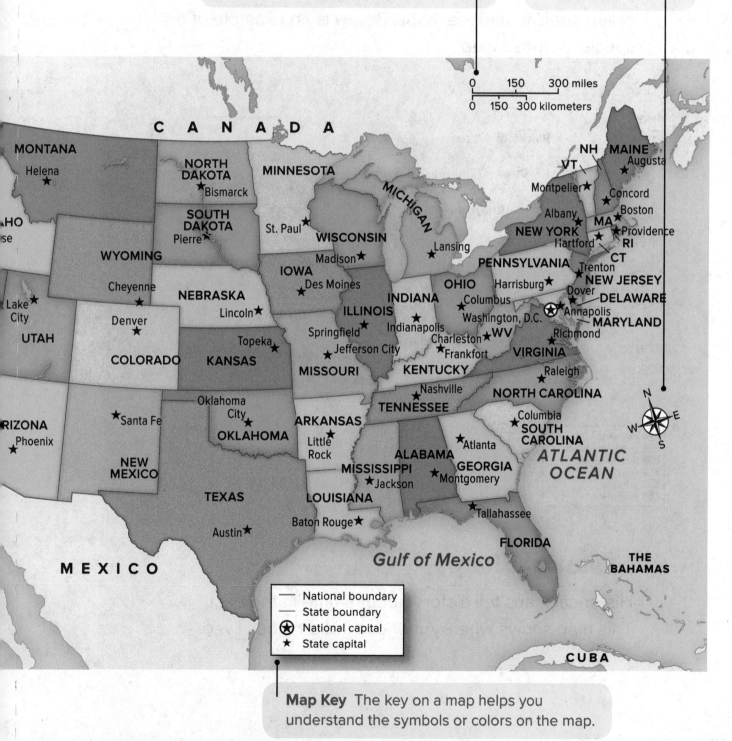

0   150   300 miles
0   150   300 kilometers

CANADA

MONTANA
Helena ★

NORTH DAKOTA
★ Bismarck

MINNESOTA

SOUTH DAKOTA
Pierre ★

St. Paul ★

WISCONSIN

MICHIGAN

Lansing ★

NH   MAINE
★ Augusta

VT
Montpelier ★   ★ Concord
★ Boston
Albany ★   MA
NEW YORK   ★ Providence
Hartford ★   RI
CT

HO
se

WYOMING

Cheyenne ★

NEBRASKA
Lincoln ★

IOWA
Des Moines ★

Madison ★

ILLINOIS

INDIANA

OHIO
Columbus ★

Harrisburg ★

PENNSYLVANIA
Trenton ★
NEW JERSEY
Dover ★ DELAWARE
Annapolis ★
MARYLAND

Lake City ★

UTAH

Denver ★

COLORADO

KANSAS
Topeka ★

MISSOURI

Springfield ★
Jefferson City ★

Indianapolis ★

Charleston ★ WV
Frankfort ★

KENTUCKY

Washington, D.C. ✪

Richmond ★

VIRGINIA

Raleigh ★

NORTH CAROLINA

Nashville ★
TENNESSEE

RIZONA
Phoenix ★

★ Santa Fe

Oklahoma City ★

OKLAHOMA

ARKANSAS
Little Rock ★

Columbia ★
SOUTH CAROLINA

Atlanta ★

ATLANTIC OCEAN

NEW MEXICO

TEXAS

Austin ★

LOUISIANA

Baton Rouge ★

MISSISSIPPI
★ Jackson

ALABAMA

Montgomery ★

GEORGIA

Tallahassee ★

N
W   E
S

MEXICO

Gulf of Mexico

FLORIDA

THE BAHAMAS

National boundary
State boundary
✪ National capital
★ State capital

CUBA

Map Key The key on a map helps you understand the symbols or colors on the map.

13a

Special Purpose Maps

Maps can show different kinds of information about an area such as how many people live there, where mountains and rivers stretch, and where the roads are. These kinds of maps detailing geographical features are called special purpose maps. Below is an example of a special purpose map.

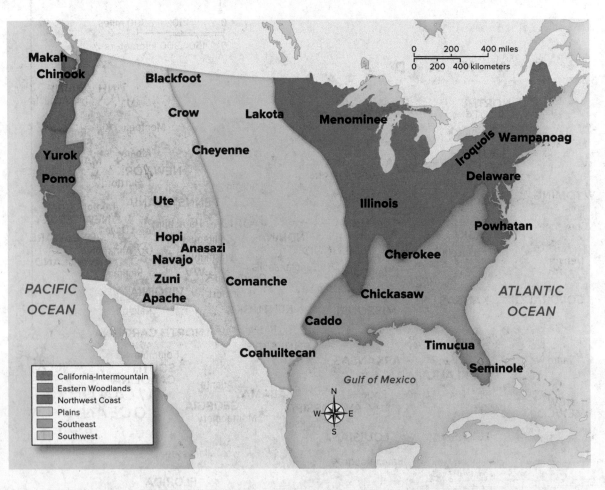

Historical Maps

Historical maps tell a story about a time in the past. This map shows where American Indian tribes lived.

Globes

A globe is a special map that is shaped like a ball. It is a small model of Earth. A model is a copy of something. A globe shows what the land and water look like on Earth.

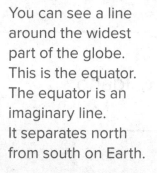

You can see a line around the widest part of the globe. This is the equator. The equator is an imaginary line. It separates north from south on Earth.

Explore Economics

The goods we buy can come from many different places. Some goods are produced locally such as fresh fruit we find at the farmer's market. Some goods come from other parts of the country such as orange juice produced in Florida. We can even purchase goods that were produced in other parts of the world such as clothes or toys made in other countries. The table below gives examples of food and where it is grown.

Food	Where it is Produced
Grapes	California
Potatoes	Idaho
Limes	Mexico

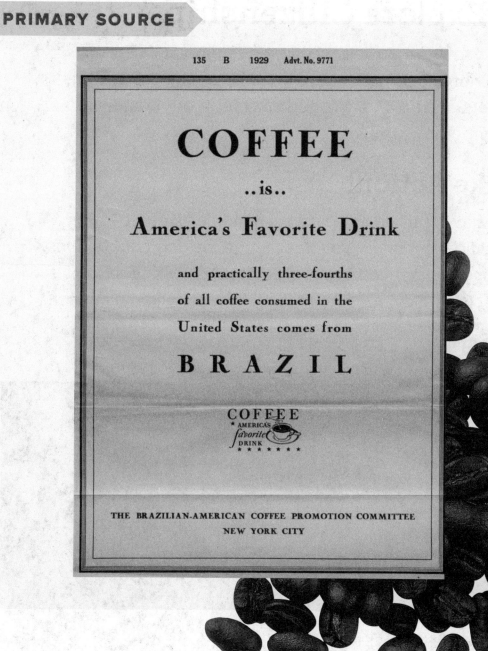

135 B 1929 Advt. No. 9771

COFFEE

..is..

America's Favorite Drink

and practically three-fourths
of all coffee consumed in the
United States comes from

B R A Z I L

COFFEE
★ AMERICA'S
favorite
DRINK
★ ★ ★ ★ ★ ★

THE BRAZILIAN-AMERICAN COFFEE PROMOTION COMMITTEE
NEW YORK CITY

Talk About It

COLLABORATE

Look closely at the picture. Where do you think these goods were produced? What details in the picture support your ideas?

Explore Citizenship

You can make an impact by being a good citizen. The words below describe good citizens. They help us understand how to be good citizens in our home, neighborhood, school, community, country, and world.

Take Action!

You have learned to be a Social Studies Detective by investigating, finding evidence, and making connections. Then you practiced investigating geography, economics, and civics. Now it's time to explore and make an impact!

PRIMARY SOURCE

The Statue of Freedom sits atop the dome of the United States Capitol.

Be a Good Citizen

COURAGE
Being brave in the face
of difficulty

FREEDOM
Making choices and holding
beliefs of one's own

HONESTY
Telling the truth

JUSTICE
Working toward fair
treatment for everyone

LEADERSHIP
Showing good behavior
worth following through
example

LOYALTY
Showing support for people
and one's country

RESPECT
Treating others as you
would like to be treated

RESPONSIBILITY
Being worthy of trust

How Does Geography Impact California Communities?

In this chapter, you will explore communities in California's four regions. You will read about the features that make these regions special. You also will learn about the ways these features affect how people live, work, and play. With a team, you will work on a chapter project to create an illustrated map of California.

Talk About It

Discuss with a partner what questions you have about communities in California.

My Research Questions

1. _____

_____

2. _____

_____

Inquiry Project

Understanding California's Geography

In this project, you will work with a team to identify California's regions and tell how geography affects the communities within them.

Here's your project checklist.

☐ **Draw** a map of California.

☐ **Identify** the state's four geographic regions.

☐ **Label** the landforms, bodies of water, and key cities, including your own.

☐ **Mark** the map with symbols to show the natural resources of each region. Then make a map key that explains what each symbol means.

☐ **Write** descriptions on index cards about the geography of each region and how it affects the lives of people who live there. Place these cards on the map.

Explore / Words

Complete this chapter's Word Rater. Write notes as you learn more about each word.

climate

☐ Know It!
☐ Heard It!
☐ Don't Know It!

My Notes

_____

_____

_____

community

☐ Know It!
☐ Heard It!
☐ Don't Know It!

My Notes

_____

_____

_____

conserve

☐ Know It!
☐ Heard It!
☐ Don't Know It!

My Notes

_____

_____

_____

elevation

☐ Know It!
☐ Heard It!
☐ Don't Know It!

My Notes

_____

_____

_____

environment

☐ Know It!
☐ Heard It!
☐ Don't Know It!

My Notes

_____

_____

_____

industry

My Notes

☐ Know It!

☐ Heard It! _____

☐ Don't Know It! _____

_____

natural resources

My Notes

☐ Know It!

☐ Heard It! _____

☐ Don't Know It! _____

_____

population

My Notes

☐ Know It! _____

☐ Heard It! _____

☐ Don't Know It! _____

_____

precipitation

My Notes

☐ Know It! _____

☐ Heard It! _____

☐ Don't Know It! _____

_____

region

My Notes

☐ Know It! _____

☐ Heard It! _____

☐ Don't Know It! _____

_____

Where Is My Community?

Lesson Outcomes

What Am I Learning?

In this lesson, you will use your investigative skills to learn more about your **community**.

Why Am I Learning It?

Reading and talking about different kinds of communities will help you understand why people choose to live in different places.

How Will I Know That I Learned It?

You will be able to describe in a paragraph the type of community where you live. You also will be able to discuss why people chose to live there.

Talk About It

COLLABORATE

Read the words to the song "I Love You, California." It is California's state song. How do the words help you understand why people would want to settle in California?

HSS.3.1.1; HAS.CS.4, HAS.HI.2

I Love You, California

I love you, California, you're the greatest state of all.

I love you in the winter, summer, spring and in the fall.

I love your fertile valleys; your dear mountains I adore.

I love your grand old ocean and I love her rugged shore.

PHOTO: Westend61/Getty Images
TEXT: Silverwood, F.B. "I Love Your, California." The California Outlook (Los Angeles and San Francisco, CA), March 22, 1913.

Julia Pfeiffer Burns State Park in Big Sur

California Counties

1 Inspect

Look at the map. What does it show?

Place a box around the following:

- The biggest county in California
- A city in Shasta County
- The county where Salinas is located

Discuss with a partner where you think your community is located.

My Notes

_____

_____

_____

_____

Did you know that your community is not just a part of the state of California? It is also a part of one of California's 58 counties. A county is a smaller area of a state. Everyone in California lives in one of these counties.

Some counties, like Los Angeles County, contain large cities. Other counties, like Alpine County or Mariposa County, have more open land and fewer people.

Just like local communities, county governments provide services. There are county roads, county schools, and county sheriffs. County offices and courts are located in the city or town that is the county seat.

Look at the map on the next page. It is called a political map. Political maps use lines, called borders, to separate counties. You can't see these lines on the land. They are imaginary lines drawn on maps to show how places are separated. Some political maps use different colors to help separate counties, too. This map also lists the county names in the map key.

2 Find Evidence

Look at the map. Which is bigger, a city or a county?

Reread How are California's counties the same? How are they different?

3 Make Connections

Talk Discuss with a partner why political maps are useful. Decide what county you live in.

COLLABORATE

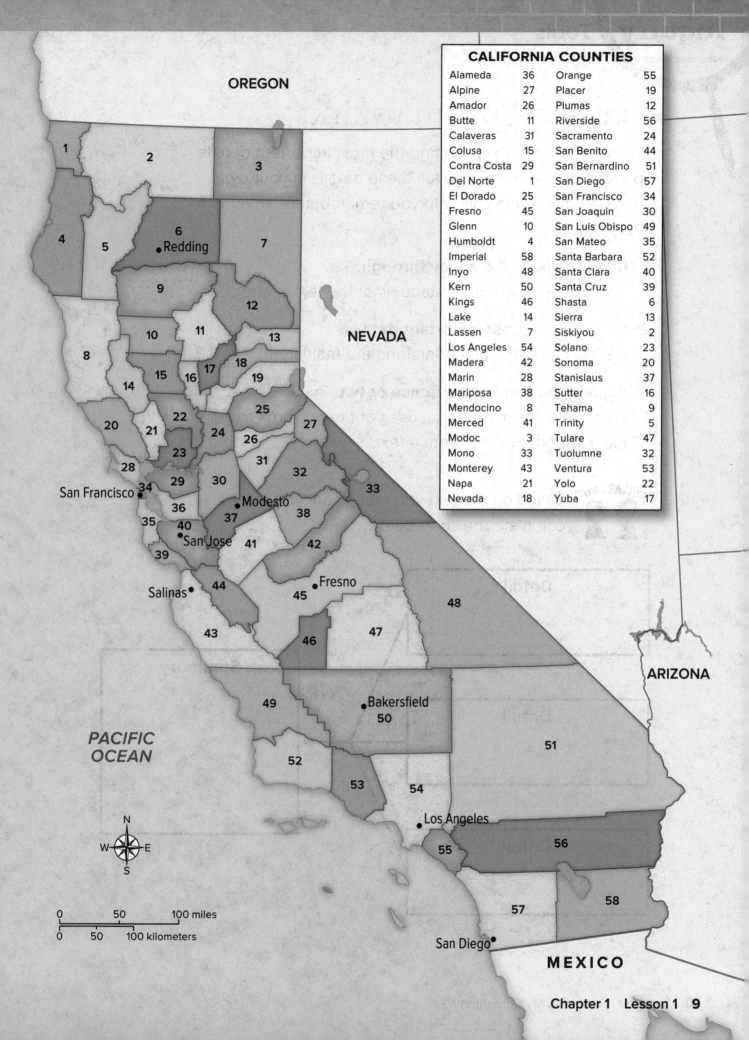

OREGON

NEVADA

CALIFORNIA COUNTIES

Alameda	36	Orange	55
Alpine	27	Placer	19
Amador	26	Plumas	12
Butte	11	Riverside	56
Calaveras	31	Sacramento	24
Colusa	15	San Benito	44
Contra Costa	29	San Bernardino	51
Del Norte	1	San Diego	57
El Dorado	25	San Francisco	34
Fresno	45	San Joaquin	30
Glenn	10	San Luis Obispo	49
Humboldt	4	San Mateo	35
Imperial	58	Santa Barbara	52
Inyo	48	Santa Clara	40
Kern	50	Santa Cruz	39
Kings	46	Shasta	6
Lake	14	Sierra	13
Lassen	7	Siskiyou	2
Los Angeles	54	Solano	23
Madera	42	Sonoma	20
Marin	28	Stanislaus	37
Mariposa	38	Sutter	16
Mendocino	8	Tehama	9
Merced	41	Trinity	5
Modoc	3	Tulare	47
Mono	33	Tuolumne	32
Monterey	43	Ventura	53
Napa	21	Yolo	22
Nevada	18	Yuba	17

Redding

San Francisco

San Jose

Salinas

Modesto

Fresno

Bakersfield

PACIFIC
OCEAN

Los Angeles

ARIZONA

San Diego

MEXICO

N
W E
S

0   50   100 miles
0   50   100 kilometers

Explain Summarizing

When you **summarize**, you find the most important details you read or see. Then, you tell these details in your own words. Summarizing can help you remember information in social studies.

1. **Read the text all the way through.**
   This will help you understand what the text is about.

2. **Look for the most important details.**
   Details can help you understand the main ideas.

3. **Explain the text in a sentence or two.**
   When you summarize, you use your own words to tell the most important ideas from a text.

 COLLABORATE Based on the text you read, work with your class to complete the chart below.

Detail

Detail

Detail

Summary

Investigate!

Read pages 6–13 in your Research Companion. Use your investigative skills to look for information to summarize what you have learned about California's communities. This chart will help you organize your notes.

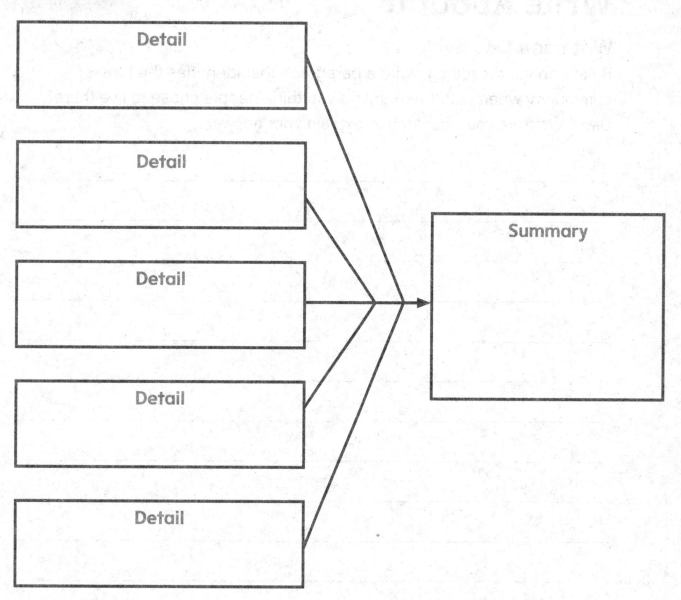

Detail

Detail

Detail

Detail

Detail

Summary

Think About It

Give an Opinion

Based on your research, what kind of community do you live in: urban, suburban, or rural? Why do you think people settled in your community?

Write About It

Write and Cite Evidence

Based on your research, write a paragraph that identifies the type of community where you live. Why do you think people chose to live there? Use facts from your research to explain your answer.

_____

_____

_____

_____

_____

_____

_____

_____

_____

_____

Talk About It

Share Your Ideas

Share your paragraph with a partner. Discuss what makes your community special.

Geography

Connect to the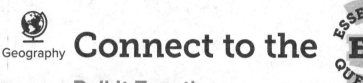

Pull It Together

Think about how geography affects California's communities. What is the geography like in your community? How does the geography affect how people live in your community?

_____

_____

_____

_____

_____

_____

 Inquiry Project Notes

_____

_____

_____

_____

_____

What Are Some Features of Each Region in California?

Lesson Outcomes

What Am I Learning?

In this lesson, you will use your investigative skills to explore the features of California's geographic **regions**.

Why Am I Learning It?

Reading and talking about California's land will help you learn more about how communities in California developed and how people live today.

How Will I Know That I Learned It?

You will be able to write a paragraph telling which region you think is most interesting and why.

desert

Talk About It

COLLABORATE

Look closely at the pictures. What do you notice? What things are the same in these pictures? What things are different?

coast

mountains

Central Valley

Parks in California

1 Inspect

Read the title. What do you think this text will be about?

- **Circle** words you do not know.
- **Underline** words that answer these questions:
  - Why do people visit California's parks?
  - Who was John Muir?

- **Discuss** with a partner why it is important to protect California's parks.

My Notes

_____

_____

_____

_____

_____

_____

_____

_____

California is home to 9 national parks. It also has many state parks and natural landmarks.

In the Central Valley, visitors can follow the California National Historic Trail. This trail once led miners and settlers into the West. Today, visitors can see historic sites such as Sutter's Fort in Sacramento.

Point Reyes National Seashore brings many visitors to California's coast each year. They come to see the sandy beaches and rocky coastline. The mountain region boasts Yosemite National Park. Yosemite is famous for high waterfalls and rocky mountain peaks.

The Mojave National Preserve is in California's desert region. It is one of the nation's largest national parks. Visitors can see mountains, canyons, and abandoned mines.

A man named John Muir worked to create laws to protect California's natural land. Some parks and landmarks in California are named after him.

PRIMARY SOURCE

In Their Words... John Muir

"But no temple made with hands can compare with Yosemite. Every rock in its wall seems to glow with life."

– *The Yosemite*, 1920

Muir, John. The Yosemite. New York: The Century Co., 1920.

Yosemite National Park covers 748,346 acres of land.

2 Find Evidence

Reread What landforms are in Point Reyes National Seashore?

Reread John Muir said the rocks "glow with life." What does this tell you about John Muir's feelings about nature?

3 Make Connections

Write a personal narrative explaining why it is important to protect the land.

John Muir explored California and wrote about its geography. In 1892, he founded the Sierra Club. He asked President Theodore Roosevelt to make laws protecting California's parks. Today, the Sierra Club still works to protect the planet and help people enjoy nature.

www.bazpics.com/Moment RF/Getty Images

Explore Main Idea and Details

The topic is what a piece of writing is about. The **main idea** is the most important point the author makes about a topic. Details tell about the main idea.

1. **Read the text once all the way through.**
   This will help you understand what the text is about.

2. **See if there is a sentence that states the main idea.**
   This is often the first sentence of a paragraph. Sometimes other sentences in a paragraph can state the main idea.

3. **Now look for details.**
   Sentences with details give more information about the main idea.

 COLLABORATE Based on the text you read, work with your class to complete the chart below.

Topic	Main Idea	Details

Investigate!

Read pages 14–23 in your Research Companion. Use your investigative skills to look for text evidence that tells you details about each of California's geographic regions. This chart will help you organize your notes.

Region	Main Idea	Details

Think About It

Gather Ideas

Based on the information you have gathered, describe each of California's geographic regions. Choose one feature from each region to describe.

Write About It

Persuade

In your opinion, which of California's geographic regions do you think is the most interesting? Why?

_____

_____

_____

_____

Write and Cite Evidence

List three reasons that support your opinion.

_____

_____

_____

_____

Talk About It

Consider Opinions

Find a classmate who chose a different region than you did. Take turns discussing your opinions and supporting evidence. Do you agree or disagree with your partner's opinion? Why?

Geography

Connect to the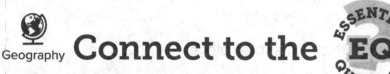

Pull It Together

Think about how the geography of California affects its communities. Why have geographers divided the state into regions?

_____

_____

_____

_____

_____

 Inquiry Project Notes

_____

_____

_____

_____

_____

What Are the Features of a Coastal Community?

Lesson Outcomes

What Am I Learning?

In this lesson, you will use your investigative skills to explore the coastal **region** of California.

Why Am I Learning It?

Reading and talking about this region will help you understand how the geography of the coastal region affects the people who live there.

How Will I Know That I Learned It?

You will be able to write a paragraph that describes the features of one of California's coastal **communities.**

COLLABORATE

Talk About It

Look closely at the picture. What type of land and water do you see? What would people do here?

raphoto/iStock/Getty Images

A coastal community at Avalon Bay on Santa Catalina Island

1 Inspect

Look Study the two photographs. What region in California do the two pictures show?

- **Discuss** with a partner the differences between the two photos.

My Notes

_____

_____

_____

_____

_____

_____

_____

_____

_____

_____

_____

_____

People exploring tide pools in Montaña de Oro State Park near Los Osos, California. California's coast has a mild climate, not too hot or too cold. Summers are cool and dry. Winters are wet and colder. In some places, the land is rocky. Rocks or cliffs go right up to the edge of the ocean.

Erica Davis/Moment/Getty Images

Beaches in southern California are warm year round. People enjoy swimming, surfing, and sunbathing.

2 Find Evidence

Review What details in the photographs help you understand the features of a coastal region?

Compare These two places are located along California's coast. What similarities do you see between these places?

3 Make Connections

Draw The two pictures show two different coastal places. Draw a picture that shows what you usually find in a coastal region.

Explore Summarizing

When you **summarize**, you explain the most important ideas and details in a text. You tell the main idea and details in your own words. A summary is shorter than the text.

1. **Read the text and look closely at any pictures.**
   This will help you understand what the text is about.

2. **Reread the text. Review the pictures. Look for the main idea.**
   Use your own words to restate the main idea.

3. **Read the text and look at the pictures again. Look for important details.**
   These details should tell more about the main idea. Add these details to your summary using your own words.

 COLLABORATE Work with your class. Use the photographs and the captions to complete the chart below.

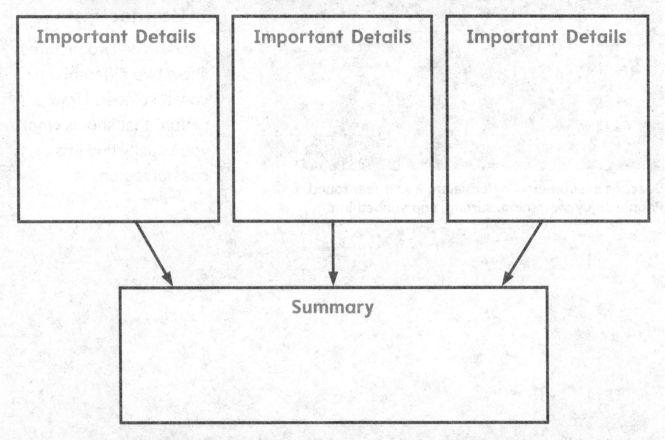

Important Details	Important Details	Important Details

Summary

Investigate!

Read pages 24–31 in your Research Companion. Use your investigative skills to look for text evidence that tells important ideas and details about California's coastal communities. Summarize what you learn. This chart will help you organize your notes for your summary.

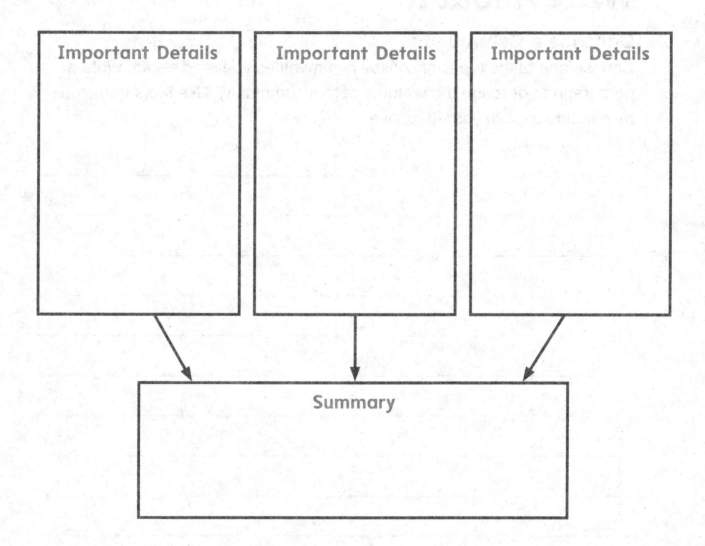

Important Details	Important Details	Important Details

Summary

Think About It

Gather Ideas

Review your research. Based on the information you have gathered, think about how you would describe the features of a coastal community to a friend.

Write About It

Describe a Community

Choose one of the types of coastal communities you read about. Write a paragraph to describe the features of that community. Use facts from your research to explain your response.

_____

_____

_____

_____

_____

_____

_____

_____

_____

_____

_____

Talk About It

Explain Your Ideas

Share your response with a partner who chose a different community.
Together, discuss the similarities and differences within coastal communities.

Geography

Connect to the

Pull It Together

Think about how geography affects California communities. How does the
ocean affect communities along California's coast?

_____

_____

_____

_____

_____

_____

 Inquiry Project Notes

_____

_____

_____

_____

_____

How Did Valley Communities Develop?

Lesson Outcomes

What Am I Learning?

In this lesson, you will use your investigative skills to explore the valley region of California.

Why Am I Learning It?

Reading and talking about this region will help you understand how the geography of California's valleys affects the people who live there.

How Will I Know That I Learned It?

You will be able to write a paragraph that describes what caused valley communities to form and change over time.

Talk About It

COLLABORATE

Look at the photograph. What type of land do you see? What information does the caption give you about farming in valleys?

HSS.3.1.1, HSS.3.1.2

Kit_Leong/iStock/Getty Images

Grapes and many other crops are grown in the Salinas Valley. Valleys have rich soil and a mild climate that are good for growing crops.

1 Inspect

Look Study the photograph carefully. What does this photograph show?

- **Draw** a box around the people.
- **Discuss** with a partner what the people are doing.

My Notes

_____

_____

_____

_____

_____

_____

_____

_____

_____

_____

_____

Brad Perks Lightscapes/Alamy

2 Find Evidence

Read the caption. What type of crop is growing? How is it being gathered?

3 Make Connections

Talk Describe this photograph to a partner. How does the photograph show what life is like in this region?

COLLABORATE

Since grapes are soft, they are often picked by hand. Then they are shipped to grocery stores across the nation.

Explore Cause and Effect

An **effect** is something that happens. A **cause** is why it happens. Signal words, such as *since*, *because*, and *as a result*, show cause and effect. You can find causes and effects in words and pictures in your social studies text.

1. **Read the text and look at any photographs.**
    This will help you understand what it is about.

2. **Understand how causes and effects are related.**
    Look for clues that show something has changed. This is the effect.

3. **Ask questions.**
    Ask: What happened? This is the effect. Ask: Why did it happen? This is the cause.

COLLABORATE Read the caption on page 33. Why are grapes picked by hand? Work with your class to complete the chart below.

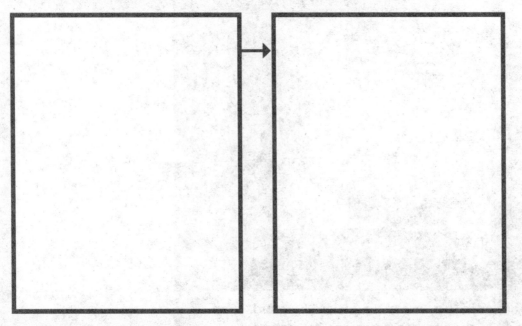

Cause   Effect

Investigate!

Read pages 32–39 in your Research Companion. Use your investigative skills to look for text evidence that shows what caused settlement in the California valley regions.

Cause	Effect
The valley soil has many minerals. The climate is mild.	
Farmers grew more food than their families needed.	
Too much or too little rain falls in the Central Valley.	
Yosemite is a beautiful park for camping, hiking, and fishing.	

Think About It

Identify Causes

Based on your research, what caused valley communities to form and change over time?

Write About It

Write and Cite Evidence

Write a paragraph that explains how valley communities formed and changed over time. Use facts from the text to explain your response.

_____

_____

_____

_____

_____

_____

_____

_____

_____

_____

_____

_____

Talk About It

Share Your Ideas

With a partner, discuss how valley communities developed and changed over time.

Geography

Connect to the

Pull It Together

Think about the geography of California valley communities. List three ways that geography affects the people who live in California's valleys.

1. _____

_____

2. _____

_____

3. _____

_____

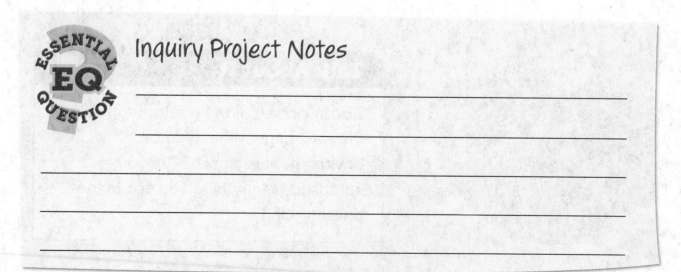

Inquiry Project Notes

_____

_____

_____

_____

_____

Lesson Outcomes

What Am I Learning?

In this lesson, you will use your investigative skills to learn about the desert **region** of California. You will also explore how the land affects the people who live there.

Why Am I Learning It?

Reading and talking about a region's **environment** will help you learn more about how geography impacts California's **communities**.

How Will I Know That I Learned It?

You will be able to write a paragraph that describes how the desert affects life for people who live there.

Talk About It

COLLABORATE

Look closely at the photograph on the next page. What type of environment is shown? Are you surprised by anything you see in the photograph?

The Anza Borrego Desert during spring bloom. Some plants thrive in the desert's harsh conditions.

1 Inspect

Look at the titles of the two graphs. What informaton is in the graphs?

- **Circle** the month with the highest average temperature in Death Valley. Then highlight the month with the greatest amount of precipitation.
- **Place a box** around the following:

  The two months that are coolest.

  The month that gets the least amount of precipitation.
- **Discuss** with a partner how the weather described in the graphs compares to the weather in your region.

My Notes

_____

_____

_____

_____

Climate Helps Describe a Region

The **climate** of a region makes a big difference! Climate is the weather a region has over a long period of time. California's coastal region has a mild climate. Summers are warm and dry. Winters are cool, short, and wet. Living in this climate can be easier than living in more extreme climates.

Imagine what it would be like to live at the North Pole. The temperatures are very cold. There is very little **precipitation**. The sun sometimes never sets and sometimes never rises. Living in this harsh climate would certainly be a challenge.

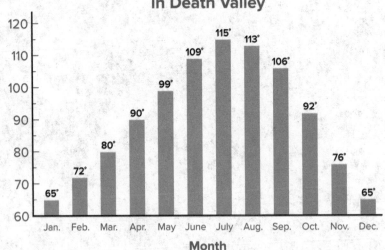

Average Monthly High Temperatures in Death Valley

Month	Temperature °F
Jan.	65°
Feb.	72°
Mar.	80°
Apr.	90°
May	99°
June	109°
July	115°
Aug.	113°
Sep.	106°
Oct.	92°
Nov.	76°
Dec.	65°

Average Monthly Precipitation in Death Valley

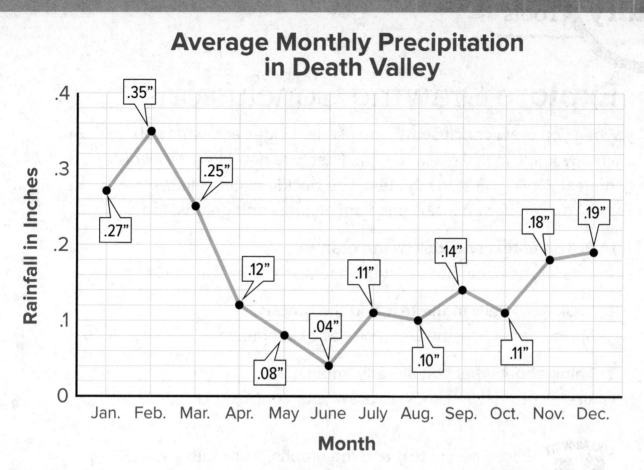

What month gets the least amount of precipitation?

California's desert can be a challenging place to live as well. A large part of southeastern California is desert. Much of this region is very hot. Its limited precipitation means there is little relief from the heat. Living in a desert can be a life-or-death situation. What would life be like if you lived there?

2 Find Evidence

Look How does the information in the graphs help you understand the environment of Death Valley?

Reread According to the text, in what way are the North Pole and the desert in California similar?

3 Make Connections

Talk Discuss with a partner the information in the graphs. How hot is 100°? How much rain is .35 inches in a month? What do you think it is like to live in Death Valley?

COLLABORATE

Explore Drawing Conclusions

When you **draw conclusions**, you use text clues and what you already know to make a judgment. First, you need to read all of the text. Once you study the text, you decide what it means to you. You can draw conclusions from pictures and graphs, too.

1. **Read the text and look at the graphs.**
   This will help you understand what the section is about.

2. **Look for details in the text and the graphs.**
   Make connections between pieces of information.

3. **Think about what you already know.**
   Use all of what you know to draw your conclusion.

 Based on the text and the graphs, work with your class to complete the chart below.

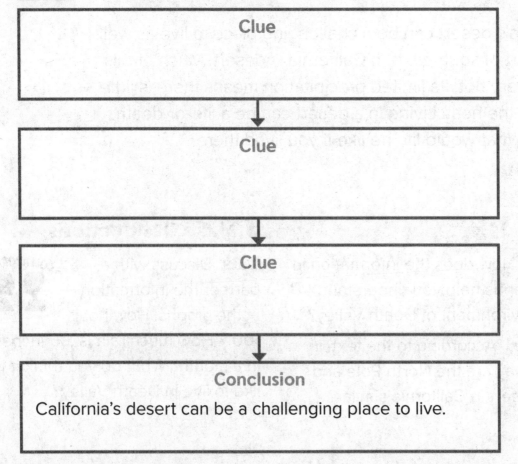

Clue

↓

Clue

↓

Clue

↓

Conclusion
California's desert can be a challenging place to live.

Investigate!

Read pages 40–47 in your Research Companion. Use your investigative skills to look for text evidence that gives you clues and helps you reach a conclusion about living in the desert. This chart will help you organize your notes.

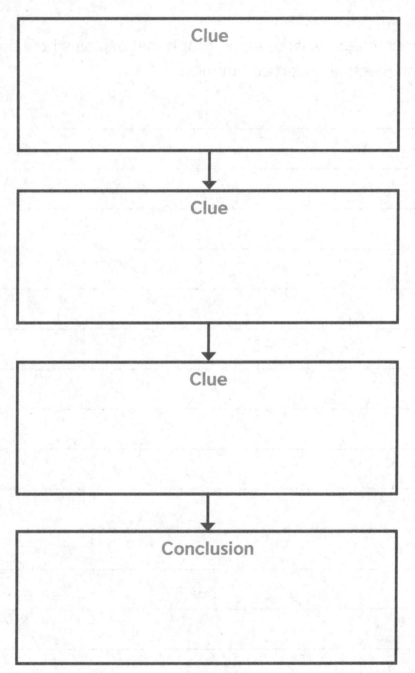

Clue

Clue

Clue

Conclusion

Think About It

Recall Details

What is it like to live in the desert?

Write About It

Write and Cite Evidence

Based on your research, write a paragraph that explains how the environment affects a desert community.

_____

_____

_____

_____

_____

_____

_____

_____

_____

_____

Talk About It

Ask Questions

Share your paragraph with a partner. Then ask and answer questions about how the environment affects life in a desert community.

Geography

Connect to the

Pull It Together

Think about how geography affects California's communities. What challenges do living things face in desert communities?

_____

_____

_____

_____

_____

_____

Inquiry Project Notes

_____

_____

_____

_____

_____

What Makes a Mountain Community Unique?

Lesson Outcomes

What Am I Learning?

In this lesson, you will use your investigative skills to understand how the land affects California's mountain **communities**.

Why Am I Learning It?

Reading and talking about the geography of a **region** will help you learn how the land affects a community.

How Will I Know That I Learned It?

You will be able to write a paragraph that describes similarities and differences in California's mountain communities.

Talk About It

COLLABORATE

Look closely at the photograph. What geographic features do you see? How would you describe the community?

Truckee, California, is in the Sierra Nevada Mountains. It averages over 200 inches of snow each year.

1 Inspect

Look at the two images. How are they similar? How are they different?

- **Circle** the geographic features that are similar in both images.
- **Discuss** with a partner which features shown in the pictures are different.

My Notes

_____

_____

_____

_____

_____

_____

_____

_____

_____

What Makes a Region Appealing?

In the 1800s, gold and silver were discovered in the California mountains. Many new settlers came to the region, hoping to get rich quickly. Towns grew because of the gold rush. More people came to open stores and build housing for the miners.

Mining began to decline over time. This caused some towns to eventually disappear. But others continued to grow as people found new ways to earn a living. Some people became shop owners. Others became skilled workers, such as carpenters or blacksmiths.

This drawing shows Placerville, California, around 1849, during the Gold Rush.

Everett Collection Historical/Alamy Stock Photo

The Old Town Bell Tower is in modern-day Placerville.
It was built in 1865 as a fire alarm.

Today, its **natural resources** still bring people to California's mountain communities. A few people hope to find gold. Most people, however, come for other reasons. Tourists come to see the beautiful landscape. Adventurers such as rock climbers and skiers come because of the **climate**.

People have chosen to live in different California communities for many reasons. A region's geography and climate are important to some. To others, it is how they can make a living or what they can do for fun. What factors are similar among all the communities of California? What factors make the mountain region unique?

2 Find Evidence

Look How do the pictures show how Placerville has changed over time?

Summarize What do you think might be an important industry in the town today?

3 Make Connections

Talk What features brought people into the mountain region in the past?

COLLABORATE

Connect to Now What features bring people to the region in the present?

Explore Compare and Contrast

To **compare** means to tell how two or more things are alike. To **contrast** means to tell how two or more things are different.

1. **Read the text all the way through.**
   This will help you understand what the text is about.

2. **Look for words that signal comparisons and contrasts.**
   Both, same, like, and *as* can help you find comparisons. *But* and *unlike* can help you find contrasts.

3. **Think about the details in the text and pictures.**
   Look for details that show how things are similar and different.

 Work with your class to complete the chart below to compare mountain communities then and now.

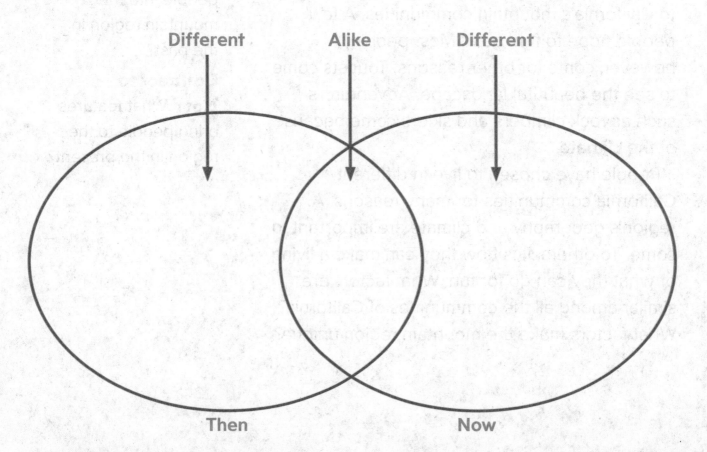

Different   Alike   Different

Then   Now

Investigate!

Read pages 48–55 in your Research Companion. Use your investigative skills to look for text evidence that compares and contrasts features of mountain communities. This chart will help you organize your notes.

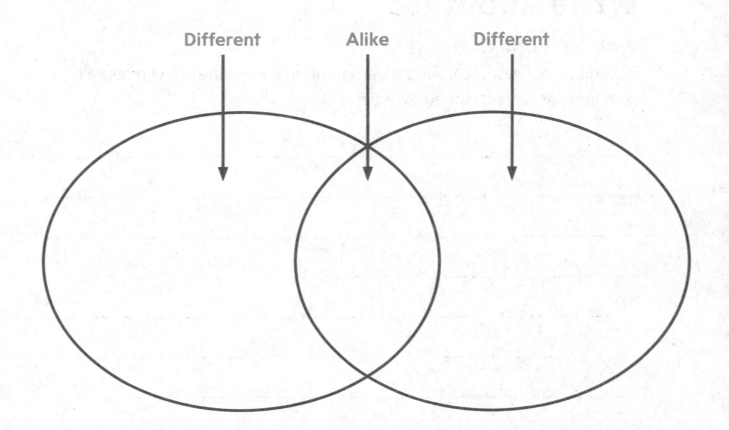

Different Alike Different

Think About It

Compare the Facts

Review your research. How have mountain communities changed over time? Use facts from your research to show similarities and differences to support your response.

Write About It

Write and Cite Evidence

Based on your research, write a paragraph that describes how mountain communities have changed over time.

_____

_____

_____

_____

_____

_____

_____

_____

_____

_____

_____

Talk About It

State the Facts

Share your response with a partner. Be sure to explain the similarities and differences you included in your writing.

Geography

Connect to the

Pull It Together

Think about how geography affects communities in California. What are some advantages and disadvantages to living in a mountain community?

_____

_____

_____

_____

_____

_____

_____

 Inquiry Project Notes

_____

_____

_____

_____

Exploring Planet Ava

CHARACTERS

Narrator
Captain Woods
Robb
Jane *(Robb and Susan's mother)*
Susan
Co-captain Carson

Three Explorers
1. Omar
2. Luke
3. Carla
Roger

National Aeronautics and Space Administration (NASA)

Narrator: It's the year 2350. A spacecraft with men, women, and children from Earth is heading to the planet Ava. Earth and planet Ava are very much alike. Ava has air and water, mountains, rivers, and good soil. Planet Ava has two natural resources that Earth does not have—Kottowool trees and a rare mineral called cordromite. The people from Earth are coming to farm Ava's Kottowool trees. They also want to mine its cordromite and send it back to Earth.

Captain Woods: Ladies and gentlemen, this is Captain Woods speaking. Please prepare for landing. Remain seated until I have turned off the seat belt sign.

Robb: Mom, why is this planet called Ava?

Jane: It was named after the nine-year-old girl who discovered it. She was looking through her telescope on Earth.

Robb: I can't wait to get outside.

Captain Woods: Okay, folks, we have come to a complete stop. Let's exit the spacecraft.

(The passengers exit the spaceship.)

Robb: *(pointing to the sky)* Look at the three moons!

Susan: Look! A Kottowool tree! Kottowool is strong and soft enough to make just about anything—clothes, rugs, sheets, pillows.

Robb: *(kicking a rock with his foot)* Here's some cordromite. That's enough to power my robotic flyer for a month!

Captain Woods: *(raising his voice to be heard)* Everyone, let's gather over here. *(All of the passengers gather around.)* We're going to set up some bio-houses here for now. By spring, we'll need to decide where to set up permanent housing before the big storms come. So let's get ready to explore.

Co-captain Carson: *(holding a digital tablet)* We have divided Ava into four regions. Each team will take a rover to explore one region. Look for natural resources, and be on the lookout for Kottowool trees and cordromite. Take video to share with the team. We'll meet back here tonight.

Narrator: The teams went in four different directions. At the end of the day, they gathered in the group living space.

NASA/JPL-Caltech

Captain Woods: Well, Team 1, what did you find today?

Omar: In our region there was a valley between two huge mountains. You can see a river that runs through it on our video.

Captain Woods: Good. We need water for drinking and washing. We also need it for the food we will grow.

Omar: The soil seems good for farming. The climate was comfortable, too.

Captain Woods: What about Kottowool trees?

Robb: *(disappointed)* We saw lots of trees but not many were Kottowool. We didn't find too much cordromite, either.

Captain Woods: Team 2, what did you find?

Susan: Our region was very hot and dry. It was a desert. There wasn't a drop of water or any Kottowool trees in sight.

Luke: We don't want to live there, sir.

Captain Woods: I agree. Team 3, you're next.

Jane: Our region has a coast. There's a beautiful beach, and two rivers empty into the ocean. We would never run out of water, that's for sure.

Susan: I would like to live near a beach! We could grow Kottowool trees.

Co-captain Carson: *(frowning)* What about cordromite?

Jane: We found some in one spot, but nowhere else.

Captain Woods: Team 4, what did you see?

Roger: *(excitedly)* Our region had mountains. Some had snow on top. There were forests of Kottowool, and our cordromite meter went nuts. There's one problem—water. There's probably not enough water for us to live and farm.

Captain Woods: That IS a problem. Is the soil rich?

Roger: Yes. We brought back soil samples. Take a look.

Image Source/Getty Images

Captain Woods: What about the climate? What's it like?

Carla: *(shrugging)* It's in the mountains, so it's cool. But it's not freezing.

Captain Woods: It sounds like a great place for us. Like the first region, it has a good climate and rich soil for farming. But it also has plenty of cordromite and Kottowool trees. How do we solve the water problem?

Roger: Captain, we could build a lake to collect and store water from rain and melted snow. Then we'll have water when we need it.

Captain Woods: Roger, that's a good plan. I think we might just name our new community "Rogersville."

Talk About It

COLLABORATE

Talk Think about the town where you live. Why do you think the people who settled there thought it would be a good place to live? Do you know how it got its name? Talk with a partner about your ideas.

Inquiry Project Wrap-Up

Understanding California's Geography

Now is the time for your team to share your illustrated map with the rest of the class. Here's what to do.

☐ Show your map. Give a brief description of each of the four regions.

☐ Explain the labels and symbols you used and why you chose to include them.

☐ Review the descriptions. Talk about how geography has affected California communities, including your own.

☐ Talk about how well you think your map describes California's features and how these features affect people's lives.

Tips for Presenting

Remember these tips when you present to your class.

☐ Make sure everyone can see your map.

☐ Take turns presenting and answering questions.

☐ Use complete sentences.

☐ Speak loudly and clearly.

Project Rubric

Use these questions to help evaluate your project.

	Yes	No
Did we identify and describe all four regions accurately?		
Were our labels and symbols clear?		
Did our descriptions make sense and provide enough information?		
Did we work well together as a team when working on the project?		
Was the whole team prepared when making our presentation?		

Project Reflection

Think about the work that you did in this chapter, either with a group or on your own. What activity did you enjoy doing the most? Why? What could you have done differently to make the other activities more enjoyable?

_____

_____

_____

_____

How Have California Indians Influenced the Local Region?

In this chapter, you will explore where and how California Indians lived in the past. You will also learn how these groups live and work today. As a class, you will work on a chapter project to make a website about the California Indian groups in your region.

Talk About It

Think about what life might have been like for California Indians in the past. Discuss this with a partner and make a list of questions you have.

My Research Questions

1. _____

   _____

2. _____

   _____

Inquiry Project

Creating a Website About California Indians

In this project, you will work with your class to create a website that tells about the past and present California Indians in your region.

Here's your project checklist.

☐ **Decide** what information to include and who your audience will be.

☐ **Determine** how the website should be organized.

☐ **Assign** each person with a specific task and give a due date.

☐ **Determine** how best to present the information you have been assigned. Would a map, chart, photographs, or a written summary tell the information best?

☐ **Conduct** research and complete the task you have been assigned.

☐ **Create** the website.

☐ **Share** your website with the audience you selected.

Explore Words

Complete this chapter's Word Rater. Write notes as you learn more about each word.

constitution   My Notes
- ☐ Know It!
- ☐ Heard It!
- ☐ Don't Know It!

culture   My Notes
- ☐ Know It!
- ☐ Heard It!
- ☐ Don't Know It!

explorer   My Notes
- ☐ Know It!
- ☐ Heard It!
- ☐ Don't Know It!

harvest   My Notes
- ☐ Know It!
- ☐ Heard It!
- ☐ Don't Know It!

migrate   My Notes
- ☐ Know It!
- ☐ Heard It!
- ☐ Don't Know It!

mission

☐ Know It!
☐ Heard It!
☐ Don't Know It!

My Notes

_____

_____

_____

nomad

☐ Know It!
☐ Heard It!
☐ Don't Know It!

My Notes

_____

_____

_____

reservation

☐ Know It!
☐ Heard It!
☐ Don't Know It!

My Notes

_____

_____

_____

traditions

☐ Know It!
☐ Heard It!
☐ Don't Know It!

My Notes

_____

_____

_____

vegetation

☐ Know It!
☐ Heard It!
☐ Don't Know It!

My Notes

_____

_____

_____

Who Lived in Early California?

Lesson Outcomes

What Am I Learning?

In this lesson, you will use your investigative skills to find out about the lives of American Indians.

Why Am I Learning It?

Reading and talking about American Indians in California will help you understand their history and **cultures**.

How Will I Know That I Learned It?

You will write a paragraph explaining how the **environment** affected the lives and cultures of American Indians in California.

Chumash Indians

Carol M. Highsmith Collection Library of Congress LC-DIG-highsm-22085

Chuck Place/Alamy

Talk About It

Look closely at the painting. What do you think was used to make the houses shown in the background?

Many Cultures

1 Inspect

Read the article and look at the title of the map. What do you think is the purpose of the map?

- **Circle** the names of the California Indian groups that lived along the coast.
- **Underline** two important ideas in the text on this page.

American Indians were the first people to live in what we now call California. They have lived here for thousands of years. They lived in different groups, each with its own culture, or way of life. Each group of California Indians had its own language, food, arts, and beliefs. The culture of each group was shaped by the environment of the region they lived in.

California Indian groups lived in all the regions of California. The map on the next page shows where some groups lived in the past. Groups such as the Ohlone and the Chumash settled along the coast. The Yokut lived in the Central Valley. The Sierra Miwok lived in the Sierra Nevada mountains. The Southern Paiute lived part of the year in the Mojave Desert.

2 Find Evidence

Draw Conclusions What do the names of some of the groups tell you about where they lived in the past?

Summarize How were California Indian groups different from each other?

_____

_____

_____

_____

3 Make Connections

Talk Discuss with a partner how you think California Indians in different regions used the resources around them.

COLLABORATE

Connect to Now Can you find a group on the map that lived close to where you live now?

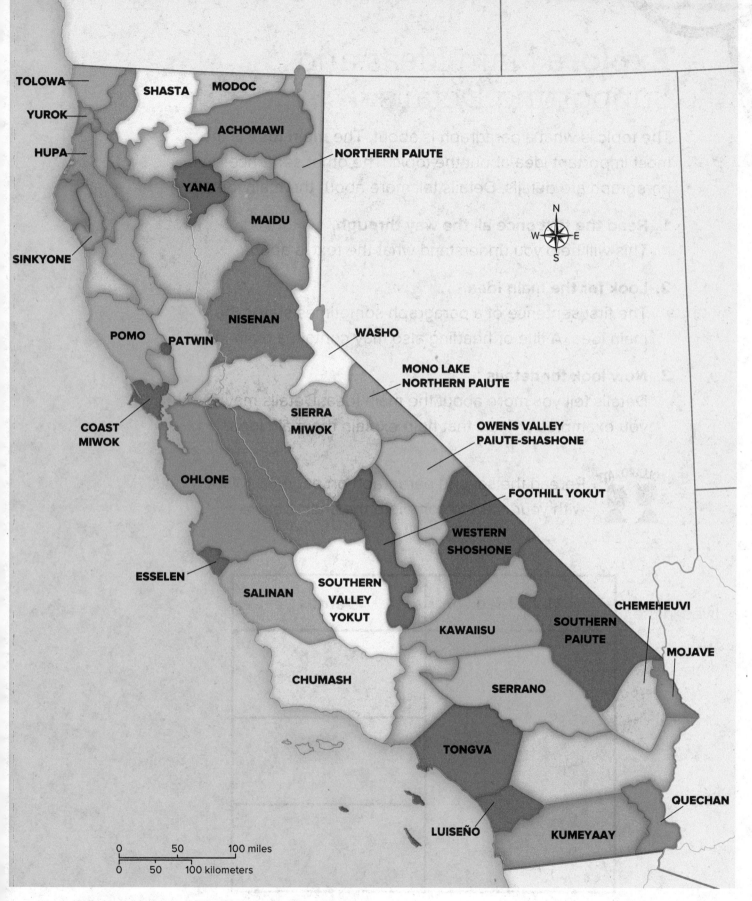

TOLOWA

YUROK

HUPA

SINKYONE

SHASTA

MODOC

ACHOMAWI

NORTHERN PAIUTE

YANA

MAIDU

NISENAN

WASHO

POMO

PATWIN

MONO LAKE
NORTHERN PAIUTE

SIERRA
MIWOK

OWENS VALLEY
PAIUTE-SHASHONE

COAST
MIWOK

OHLONE

FOOTHILL YOKUT

WESTERN
SHOSHONE

ESSELEN

SALINAN

SOUTHERN
VALLEY
YOKUT

CHEMEHEUVI

SOUTHERN
PAIUTE

KAWAIISU

MOJAVE

CHUMASH

SERRANO

TONGVA

QUECHAN

LUISEÑO

KUMEYAAY

0   50   100 miles

0   50   100 kilometers

Original Homes of California Indian Groups

Explore Main Ideas and Supporting Details

The topic is what a paragraph is about. The **main idea** is the most important idea about the topic. The other sentences in a paragraph are details. Details tell more about the main idea.

1. **Read the text once all the way through.**
   This will help you understand what the text is about.

2. **Look for the main idea.**
   The first sentence of a paragraph sometimes states the main idea. A title or heading also may contain a main idea.

3. **Now look for details.**
   Details tell you more about the main idea. Details may give you examples or facts that help explain the main idea.

 COLLABORATE Reread the second paragraph on page 68. Work with your class to complete the chart below.

Main Idea	Details

Investigate!

Read pages 64–71 in your Research Companion. Use your investigative skills to look for main ideas and details that help you understand the people who lived in early California. This chart will help you organize your notes.

Main Ideas	Details

Think About It

Gather Ideas

Review your research. Based on the information you have gathered, how did the land affect California Indians?

Write About It

Write and Cite Evidence

What factors influenced the lives of California Indians?

_____

_____

_____

_____

_____

_____

_____

_____

_____

_____

_____

_____

Talk About It

Consider Different Ideas

Share your response with a partner. Discuss the factors you wrote about and how they influenced the cultures of California Indians.

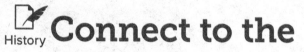

Connect to the EQ

History

Pull It Together

How were California Indians influenced by the regions in which they lived?

_____

_____

_____

_____

_____

_____

_____

_____

Inquiry Project Notes

_____

_____

_____

_____

How Did the Land Affect California Indians?

Lesson Outcomes

What Am I Learning?

In this lesson, you will use your investigative skills to explore how California Indians were affected by their surroundings.

Why Am I Learning It?

Reading and talking about different climates and landforms will help you understand how California Indians adapted to their surroundings.

How Will I Know That I Learned It?

You will be able to write a paragraph that describes how the environment affected the daily lives of California Indians who lived there.

Talk About It

COLLABORATE

Look closely at the photograph. What does the land look like? What natural resources do you see? What do you think it would be like to live there?

HSS.3.1.1, HSS.3.1.2, HAS.CS.4

A view of Yosemite Valley

1 Inspect

Look at the map's title. What does the map show you?

- **Circle** in the key two types of plants that are most widespread in California.
- **Underline** in the key the type of plant found in the southeast part of California.
- **Discuss** with a partner what types of plants are found in your community.

My Notes

_____

_____

_____

A Land of Rich Vegetation

California has a variety of **vegetation**, or plant life, across the state. The map shows the most common types of vegetation in different regions of the state.

The northern and central part of the state is rich in forests. The Central Valley region has grasses that grow in the rich soil. Farther south, only desert plants grow in the desert's hot and dry climate.

California Indian groups used the vegetation of their regions in many ways. Groups that lived in northern areas used trees to make their homes and boats. Groups that lived in the Central Valley used grasses to make homes and boats. Each group used what was available in their environment.

2 Find Evidence

Look What region or regions do you think has the most natural resources?

_____

_____

Circle the region where you live today. How would you describe your region's environment?

_____

_____

3 Make Connections

Talk With a partner, talk about the types of plants shown on the map key. Explain how you think the plants may have been used by the California Indians in each region.

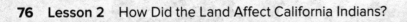
COLLABORATE

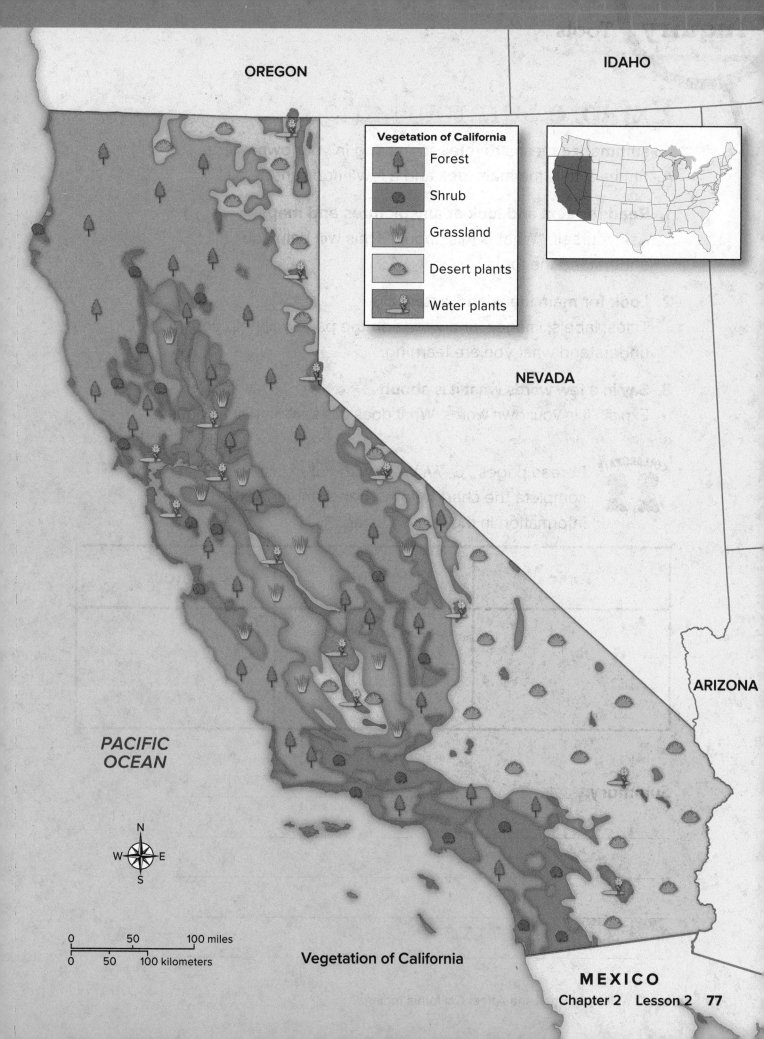

OREGON

IDAHO

Vegetation of California

🌲 Forest

🌵 Shrub

🌾 Grassland

🌿 Desert plants

🌸 Water plants

NEVADA

ARIZONA

PACIFIC
OCEAN

N
W E
S

0   50   100 miles
0   50   100 kilometers

Vegetation of California

MEXICO

Explore Summarizing

To **summarize** means to retell something in your own words. A summary tells the main idea and a few important details.

1. **Read the text and look at any pictures and maps.**
   Ask yourself, "What is this about?" This will help you understand the topic.

2. **Look for main ideas and details.**
   Titles, labels, images, and words on the page will help you understand what you are learning.

3. **Say in a few words what it is about.**
   Explain it in your own words. What does this section teach you?

COLLABORATE Reread pages 76–77. Work with your class to complete the chart below. Then summarize the information in the text and map.

Topic	Main Idea	Details

Summary: _____

_____

_____

_____

Investigate!

Read pages 72–77 in your Research Companion. Use your investigative skills to look for text evidence that helps you understand the main topic. The text evidence will include main ideas and details. This chart will help you organize your notes.

Topic	Main Idea	Details

Summary: _____

_____

_____

Think About It

Research

Based on your research, what California Indians lived in your region? Use maps and text evidence to support your answer.

Write About It

Write and Cite Evidence

Choose one region that you learned about. Write a paragraph to explain in your own words how the environment affected the California Indians who lived there.

_____

_____

_____

_____

_____

_____

_____

_____

_____

_____

_____

Talk About It

Explain

Share your answers with a partner. Discuss how the land and climate in another region of California affected the California Indians who lived there.

Geography

Connect to the

Pull It Together

What effects did a region's environment have on the daily life of California Indians?

_____

_____

_____

_____

_____

 Inquiry Project Notes

_____

_____

_____

_____

_____

_____

How Did California Indians Change the Land?

Lesson Outcomes

What Am I Learning?

In this lesson, you will use your investigative skills to explore how and why California Indians changed the land around them.

Why Am I Learning It?

Reading and talking about how California Indians changed the land will help you learn more about how they lived.

How Will I Know That I Learned It?

You will write a paragraph to explain why and how the California Indians in your region changed their environment to meet their needs.

Talk About It

COLLABORATE

Look closely at the photograph. How would you describe this fire?

HSS.3.1.2, HAS.HI.3

Naskigoard/Shutterstock.com

Some California Indian groups used fire to clear
the land for planting crops.

Working with the Land

Read Look at the title. What do you think this section will be about?

- **Circle** words you don't know.
- **Underline** things the Kumeyaay did that might have changed the land.
- **Discuss** with a partner how this text explains how the Kumeyaay made the land around them work better.

My Notes

_____

_____

_____

_____

_____

_____

_____

_____

_____

One group of California Indians who worked with their land was the Kumeyaay. The Kumeyaay have lived in what is now San Diego County for thousands of years. Long ago, they changed the land to grow food.

The Kumeyaay learned that some plants grew well after a forest fire. The Kumeyaay started fires. These fires cleared the land. This provided space for new plants to grow. They used these plants for food and medicine. In this way, the Kumeyaay changed the land around them.

Another way the Kumeyaay changed the land was to build dams. They used rocks and sticks to guide water to certain areas of the land. They also used dams to slow down the flow of water. When the water moved too fast, it washed away the soil. Because the dams slowed down the water, the Kumeyaay could use the soil for farming.

Bob Nichols/USDA-ARS

A trout trap helped California Indians catch a lot of fish.

2 Find Evidence

Look Describe in your own words how the Kumeyaay changed the land. Why did they do this?

Connect Do you think other California Indian groups had to change their land? Why?

3 Make Connections

Talk How does this picture relate to the text? How do these sources help you to understand why California Indians made changes to the land?

COLLABORATE

Explore Cause and Effect

An **effect** is something that happens. A **cause** is why it happens. Here's an example: *Because it rained* (cause), *the field was muddy* (effect). Understanding cause and effect can give you a better understanding of events in history.

1. **Look for clue words when you read the text.**
   Authors sometimes use clue words such as *because, so,* and *since* to signal causes and effects.

2. **Ask questions.**
   Asking what happened and why it happened can help you find causes and effects.

3. **Reread the text to understand what is happening.**
   Once you've identified causes and effects in a text, you'll have a deeper understanding of what you read.

 COLLABORATE Reread page 84. Work with your class to find a cause and effect. Complete the chart below.

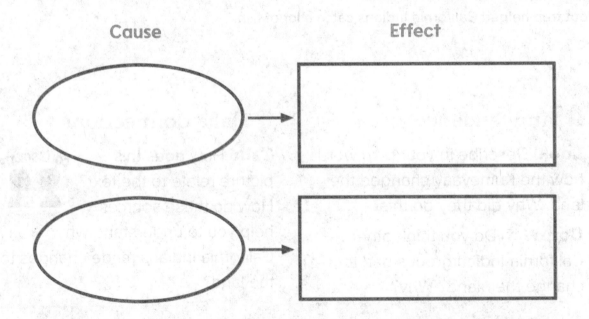

Cause   Effect

Investigate!

Read pages 78–83 in your Research Companion. Use your investigative skills to look for text clues that show what happened (causes) and the results (effects). This chart will help you organize your notes.

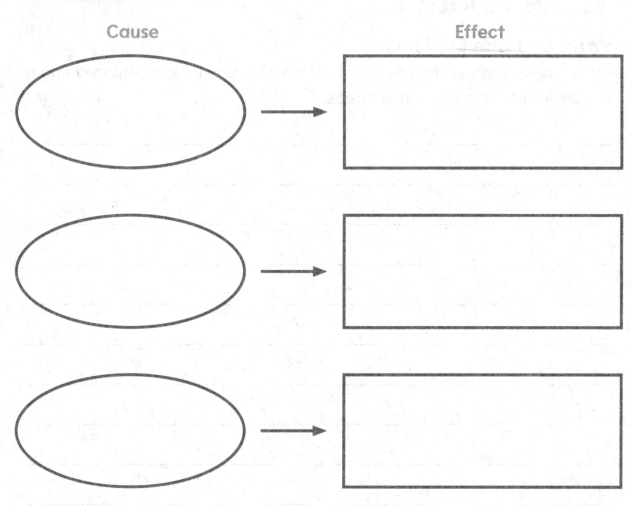

Cause   Effect

Think About It

Gather Ideas

Based on your research, how do you think California Indians from your region lived long ago?

Write About It

Write and Cite Evidence

Write a paragraph describing how California Indians in your region changed the environment to meet their needs.

_____

_____

_____

_____

_____

_____

_____

_____

_____

_____

Talk About It

Express Your Opinion

Share your writing with a partner. What change to the land do you think was most important? Why?

Geography

Connect to the

Explain

How did the changes to the land made by California Indians long ago affect your region today?

_____

_____

_____

_____

_____

_____

 Inquiry Project Notes

_____

_____

_____

_____

_____

How Did California Indians Use Natural Resources?

Lesson Outcomes

What Am I Learning?

In this lesson, you will use your investigative skills to find out how California Indians used natural resources.

Why Am I Learning It?

Reading and talking about how California Indians used resources will help you learn more about how they lived.

How Will I Know That I Learned It?

You will be able to write about how California Indians in your region used natural resources for food, clothing, shelter, tools, and trade.

Talk About It

COLLABORATE

Look at the photograph of a willow tree and read the quotation on the next page. How does Jane Dumas say we use willow trees? What other ways do we use plants and trees?

HSS.G.2.1, HSS.3.2.2

PRIMARY SOURCE

In Their Words... Jane Dumas

"A lot of plants ... have meaning to people. The willow gives us clothes to wear, the wood to build our homes, and aspirin comes from the willow."

—Jane Dumas, Kumeyaay elder

Using Natural Resources

1 Inspect

Read the text. What is it about?

- **Underline** a question the article asks you to consider.
- **Circle** details that tell you what kinds of things you would need to find if you lived in a place with no stores.
- **Discuss** with a partner what natural resources the woman in the photo is using.

My Notes

_____

_____

_____

What if you lived in a place with no stores or restaurants? Instead of shopping for your dinner, you would have to find your food in the environment. You would need to know which plants were safe to eat and how to gather them. You would have to understand how to fish and how to hunt. Your food and shelter, and even the tools you used, would be shaped by the natural resources around you.

This is how California Indians lived. They adapted to their environment and used natural resources for food, shelter, tools, and transportation. What would this be like for you?

Imagine that you couldn't buy what you needed at a store. What resources from your environment could you use for food, shelter, tools, and transportation in the region where you live?

2 Find Evidence

Look The photo shows a woman gathering seeds. How is she using the resources around her? What can you tell about the tools she is using?

3 Make Connections

Talk Discuss with a partner what it would be like to have to depend on the resources around you. Would it be easy or difficult? Why?

COLLABORATE

A coastal Pomo Indian woman gathering seeds.

Explore Main Idea and Details

The **main idea** is the most important point the author makes about a topic. Key details tell about the main idea.

1. **Read the text all the way through.**
   Pay attention to the images, captions, and headings.

2. **Reread the text and look for the most important idea.**
   This is the main idea.

3. **Look for details that tell about the main idea.**

 COLLABORATE

What is the main idea of "Using Natural Resources"? Work with your class to complete the chart below.

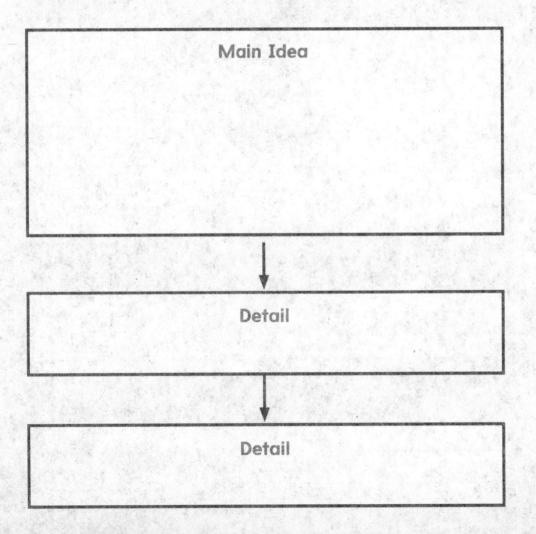

Main Idea

Detail

Detail

Investigate!

Read pages 84–91 in your Research Companion. Use your investigative skills to look for text evidence that tells you the main idea and the details. This chart will help you organize your notes.

Main Idea

↓

Detail

↓

Detail

↓

Detail

Think About It

Examine

Based on your research, what resources in your local region were important to California Indians?

Write About It

Describe

Write two or three sentences that tell how California Indians in your region used natural resources for some of the following: food, clothing, shelter, tools, transportation, and trade.

_____

_____

_____

_____

_____

_____

_____

_____

_____

_____

Talk About It

Discuss

Share your writing with a partner. Discuss how the natural resources in your local region affected the way California Indians lived.

Geography

Connect to the

Pull It Together

How did California Indians use local resources in their lives?

_____

_____

_____

_____

_____

 Inquiry Project Notes

_____

_____

_____

_____

_____

What Defines a California Indian Community?

Lesson Outcomes

What Am I Learning?

In this lesson, you will use your investigative skills to explore the **cultures** of today's California Indian communities.

Why Am I Learning It?

Reading and talking about these communities will help you understand their impact on California.

How Will I Know That I Learned It?

You will be able to write a paragraph that describes how California Indian communities keep their cultures alive and continue to share their **traditions**.

Talk About It

COLLABORATE

Look closely at the picture. What do you see? What do you think the children are learning?

California Indian adults pass down their traditions to children. They teach important values, tell the old stories, sing songs, and play music.

Putnam, Frederic Ward. "Yaudanchi Yokuts. The Origin of Fire." American Archaeology and Ethnology. Berkeley: Berkeley University Press, 1906-1907.

1 Inspect

Read Look at the title. What do you think this story will be about? Read the story.

- **Circle** words you don't know.
- **Underline** clues that help you identify the hero of the story.
- **Discuss** with a partner why this story should be read aloud by a storyteller.

My Notes

_____

_____

_____

_____

_____

_____

_____

_____

The Origin of Fire (A Yaudancchi Yokut Legend)

This story is a retelling. It explains how fire was brought to the Yokut people. Stories such as this were told to help explain things that happened in nature.

The people in the foothills had no fire. There was a man who lived in the plains. He had all the fire.

When he slept, an antelope went to steal his fire. The antelope could run fast. He picked up the fire and ran. The antelope stayed out in the open grass with the fire. A heavy rain came and put out the fire.

Other animals tried to steal the fire, but they could not. The last one to steal the fire was the jackrabbit. After he stole the fire, he hid in the bushes. He crouched over the fire, holding it in his hands near his belly. This is why the jackrabbit has black paws. Because the jackrabbit protected the fire, he was able to safely bring it to his people in the foothills.

The jackrabbit stole the fire and carried it away.

2 Find Evidence

Reread What is the purpose of this story?

Reread the statement, "He crouched over the fire, holding it in his hands near his belly." How did that look? Think of a word that has the same meaning as *crouched*.

3 Make Connections

Talk Discuss with a partner the meaning of this story. Stories that are passed down in a community often tell what is important. What does this story say is important? How do you know?

COLLABORATE

Explore Summarizing

When you **summarize**, you tell the most important ideas and details. Summarizing can help you remember what you read.

1. **Read the text all the way through.**
   This will help you understand what it is about.

2. **Look for the main idea or the most important events.**
   Restate the main idea or events in your own words.

3. **Reread the text and look for important details.**
   Add only the most important details to your summary.

4. **Retell the text in your own words.**
   Use the main idea and details in your summary.

 COLLABORATE Work with your class to complete the chart and write a summary of the story "The Origin of Fire."

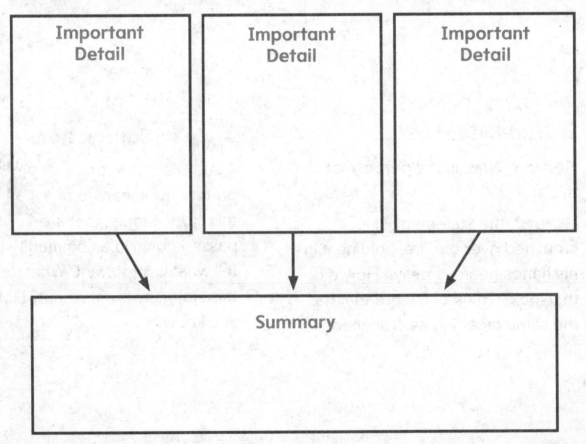

Important Detail	Important Detail	Important Detail

Summary

Investigate!

Read pages 92–97 in your Research Companion. Use your investigative skills to look for text evidence that helps you summarize information about California Indian communities. This chart will help you organize your notes.

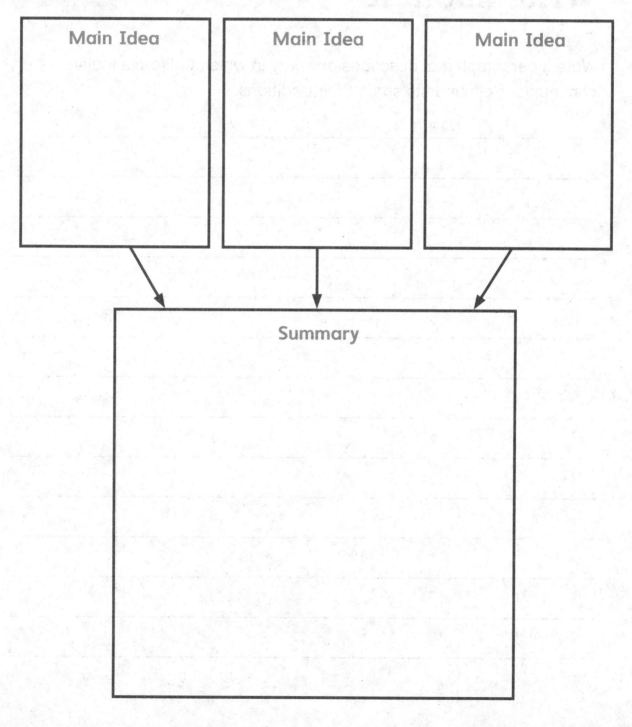

Main Idea

Main Idea

Main Idea

Summary

Think About It

Identify

Based on your research, what are some ways California Indians keep their cultures alive?

Write About It

Explain

Write a paragraph that describes one way in which California Indian communities continue to share their traditions.

_____

_____

_____

_____

_____

_____

_____

_____

_____

_____

_____

Talk About It

COLLABORATE

Explain

Share your writing with a partner. Discuss other ways California Indian communities share their traditions.

 Geography

Connect to the

ESSENTIAL QUESTION

Pull It Together

How do you see influences of California Indian communities in your life today?

_____

_____

_____

_____

_____

 Inquiry Project Notes

_____

_____

_____

_____

_____

How Do California Indian Communities Work?

Lesson Outcomes

What Am I Learning?

In this lesson, you will use your investigative skills to learn about the economy and government of California Indian groups.

Why Am I Learning It?

Reading and talking about the economy and government will help you understand more about California Indian communities.

How Will I Know That I Learned It?

You will be able to write a paragraph that explains how California Indian governments are organized.

Talk About It

COLLABORATE

Look closely at the picture on the top of the next page. What type of meeting do you think this is?

HSS.3.2.1, HSS.3.2.3

The Yurok tribal council worked with the federal government to clean up pollution in the Klamath River.

Leading the Kumeyaay

Look at the title. What do you think the text is about?

- **Circle** the number of people in a band.
- **Underline** the text that explains why the Kumeyaay worked out a plan for government.
- **Discuss** with a partner how the Kumeyaay government worked. Would you want to be a captain or a council member? Why or why not?

My Notes

_____

_____

_____

_____

_____

_____

_____

_____

The Kumeyaay Indians lived on a large area of land. The Kumeyaay people lived in small groups called bands. Each band had its own land and the right to use the natural resources on it. Because they had so many people and such a large territory, the Kumeyaay worked out a plan for government.

Kumeyaay land was divided into regions. Each region had a general who was in charge of the bands who lived there. A band could have 200 people or as many as 1,000 people. Each band had a leader called a captain. Captains might be born into the position, or they might be chosen because they were good leaders.

Each captain had a council. A council is a group of people who work with a leader to make decisions. These leaders made decisions such as when the band should move or how to protect an important food source. They sometimes decided if it was necessary to go to war.

Each band had a central village where the leader and his council lived. Important ceremonies were also held there.

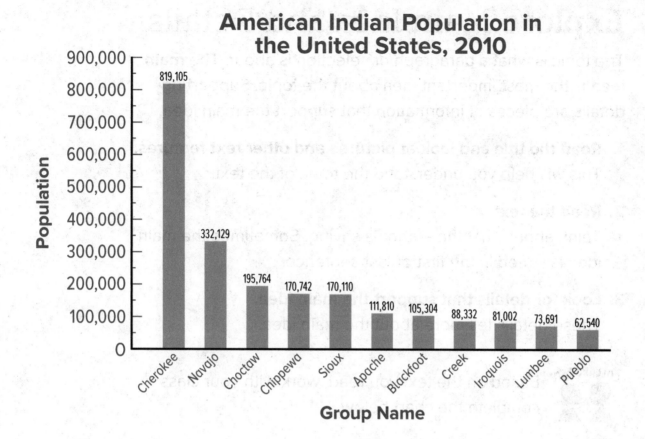

American Indian Population in the United States, 2010

Population (y-axis), Group Name (x-axis)

- Cherokee: 819,105
- Navajo: 332,129
- Choctaw: 195,764
- Chippewa: 170,742
- Sioux: 170,110
- Apache: 111,810
- Blackfoot: 105,304
- Creek: 88,332
- Iroquois: 81,002
- Lumbee: 73,691
- Pueblo: 62,540

2 Find Evidence

Reread Why did the Kumeyaay set up a government? Look for details that tell how the Kumeyaay government was set up.

Look at the graph above. Which American Indian group is the largest in the U.S. today?

3 Make Connections

Talk Discuss with a partner how you think the Kumeyaay's government helped them. Does any part of the Kumeyaay government remind you of the way the United States government is set up today?

COLLABORATE

Explore Main Idea and Details

The topic is what a paragraph or selection is about. The **main idea** is the most important idea about the topic. Supporting details are pieces of information that support the main idea.

1. **Read the title and look at pictures and other text features.**
   This will help you understand the topic of the text.

2. **Read the text.**
   Think about what the author is saying. Sometimes the main idea is stated in the first or last sentence.

3. **Look for details that support the main idea.**
   These details tell more about the main idea.

 COLLABORATE Based on the text you read, work with your class to complete the chart below.

Main Idea	Details

Investigate!

Read pages 98–105 in your Research Companion. Use your investigative skills to explore more about how California Indian communities are organized. Use the chart to organize information.

Main Idea	Details

Think About It

Examine

Based on your research, why do California Indians still have their own governments today?

Write About It

Write and Cite Evidence

Write a paragraph that explains how California Indian governments are organized.

_____

_____

_____

_____

_____

_____

_____

_____

_____

_____

_____

_____

_____

Talk About It

COLLABORATE

Discuss

Talk to a classmate about how California Indian governments work today. What services do they provide to their tribes?

Geography

Connect to the EQ

ESSENTIAL QUESTION

Pull It Together

Why is it important to learn about the organization of California Indian governments?

_____

_____

_____

_____

_____

_____

ESSENTIAL QUESTION

EQ

Inquiry Project Notes

_____

_____

_____

_____

_____

_____

Inquiry Project Wrap-Up

Creating a Website About California Indians

Now is the time for your class to finalize and share the website. Here's what to do.

☐ Review the information on your website. Decide if you need to make changes.

☐ Make sure all the information you created can be seen on the website and is placed correctly.

☐ Share the website with your school or community.

Tips for Creating a Website

Remember these tips when you create and share a website.

☐ Make sure the information you are responsible for is accurate, clear, and engaging.

☐ Listen to feedback from your classmates and make changes as needed.

☐ Be patient and helpful as you work with your classmates.

☐ Have fun!

Project Rubric

Use these questions to help evaluate your project.

	Yes	No
Was your task done well and completed on time?		
Did the way you presented your information work?		
Did the structure of the website make sense?		
Did the class collaborate and work well together?		
Was the audience's response to the website positive?		

Project Reflection

Think about the work that you did in this chapter, either with a group or on your own. Describe something that you are most proud of. What could you have done differently to make the website better?

_____

_____

_____

_____

Chapter 3

How and Why Communities Change Over Time

How Has Life Changed for People in My Community Over Time?

In this chapter, you will explore how and why communities grow. You will learn about how people have settled and changed California's communities. You will also read about what makes these communities special. With a small group, you will work on a chapter project to make a timeline describing the development of your community.

Talk About It

Discuss with a partner what questions you have about how communities grow and change.

My Research Questions

1. _____

   _____

2. _____

   _____

EQ Inquiry Project

Sequencing Your Community's Development

In this project, you'll work with a small group to create a timeline showing the sequence of key events that played a role in the development of your community.

Here's your project checklist.

☐ **Research** the history of your community.

☐ **Choose** key events that affected the growth of your community.

☐ **Identify** locations in your community where some of these key events took place.

☐ **Write** a description of each event and place. Tell why it helped your community grow.

☐ **Find** images to use with each description.

☐ **Create** an illustrated timeline with your descriptions and images, showing these events in the order they occurred.

Explore Words

Complete this chapter's Word Rater. Write notes as you learn more about each word.

aqueduct

My Notes

☐ Know It!
☐ Heard It!
☐ Don't Know It!

_____
_____
_____

century

My Notes

☐ Know It!
☐ Heard It!
☐ Don't Know It!

_____
_____
_____

decade

My Notes

☐ Know It!
☐ Heard It!
☐ Don't Know It!

_____
_____
_____

drought

My Notes

☐ Know It!
☐ Heard It!
☐ Don't Know It!

_____
_____
_____

entrepreneur

My Notes

☐ Know It!
☐ Heard It!
☐ Don't Know It!

_____
_____
_____

ethnic group

My Notes

☐ Know It!

☐ Heard It!

☐ Don't Know It!

_____

_____

_____

expedition

My Notes

☐ Know It!

☐ Heard It!

☐ Don't Know It!

_____

_____

_____

innovation

My Notes

☐ Know It!

☐ Heard It!

☐ Don't Know It!

_____

_____

_____

pollution

My Notes

☐ Know It!

☐ Heard It!

☐ Don't Know It!

_____

_____

_____

settlers

My Notes

☐ Know It!

☐ Heard It!

☐ Don't Know It!

_____

_____

_____

Why Do People Move to a New Region?

Lesson Outcomes

What Am I Learning?

In this lesson, you will use your investigative skills to find out why people move to a new region.

Why Am I Learning It?

Reading and talking about people who have moved to a new region will help you understand the reasons why people decide to move to a new place.

How Will I Know That I Learned It?

You will write a paragraph explaining the main reason people move to a new place.

Talk About It

COLLABORATE

Look at the photograph on the next page. When do you think this photo was taken? What words would you use to describe the people in the photo?

HSS.3.3.1, HSS.3.3.3, HAS.CS.3, HAS.HI.2, HAS.HI.3

People moving to California to escape the drought in Oklahoma.

1 Inspect

Look at the graph. What does it show?

Circle the year when California's population was almost 20 million.

Place a box around the following:

- the point on the graph showing the population in 1950
- the point on the graph showing the population in 2000

My Notes

_____

_____

_____

_____

_____

_____

_____

_____

_____

California, Here We Come!

Why did so many people migrate to California between 1950 and 2010? One reason is the climate. You've read that much of California has a warm climate. People came to the state to enjoy good weather all year.

Another reason people moved to California was for jobs. In the 1940s, the United States was fighting in a war. Many people came to the state to work on military bases. Other people came to help build airplanes and ships. After the war ended, many of these people stayed in California.

In the 1950s and 1960s, lots of people came to California to work in factories in the state. People also came to do research and work in education. In the 1970s, California became a center of the technology industry. Between 1950 and 2010, people also came to work on farms in the state.

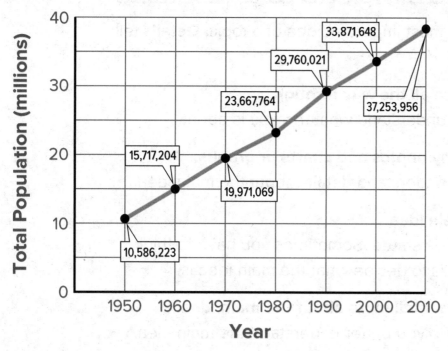

California's Population, 1950–2010

Total Population (millions) vs **Year**

- 10,586,223
- 15,717,204
- 19,971,069
- 23,667,764
- 29,760,021
- 33,871,648
- 37,253,956

How to Read a Line Graph

A line graph shows information that changes over time. To read a line graph, look at the graph's title and the labels. These tell you what the graph is about. The points, or dots, on the line show the information for each year. Trace the line connecting the points to see changes over time. On this graph, the line goes up. This means the population has grown.

2 Find Evidence

Reread Look at the points for 1950 and 2010. What happened to California's population during this time?

How many more people lived in California in 1990 than in 1970?

3 Make Connections

Talk Discuss with a partner how the graph supports the main idea of the article.

COLLABORATE

Explore Main Ideas and Details

The **main idea** is the most important idea of a topic. **Details** tell more about the main idea.

1. **Read the text once all the way through.**
   This will help you understand what the text is about.

2. **Look closely at any photos and charts or graphs.**
   This will help you understand details about the main idea.

3. **Decide on the main idea.**
   It may or may not be stated. Sometimes you have to think about all the details to decide what the main idea is.

4. **Look for details that tell more about the main idea.**
   The details will help you better understand the main idea.

COLLABORATE Based on what you have read so far, work with your class to complete the web below.

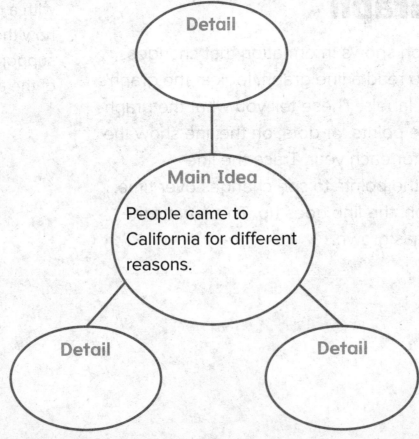

Detail

Main Idea

People came to California for different reasons.

Detail

Detail

Investigate!

Read pages 114–119 in your Research Companion. Use your investigative skills to look for details that support the main idea. This web will help you organize your notes.

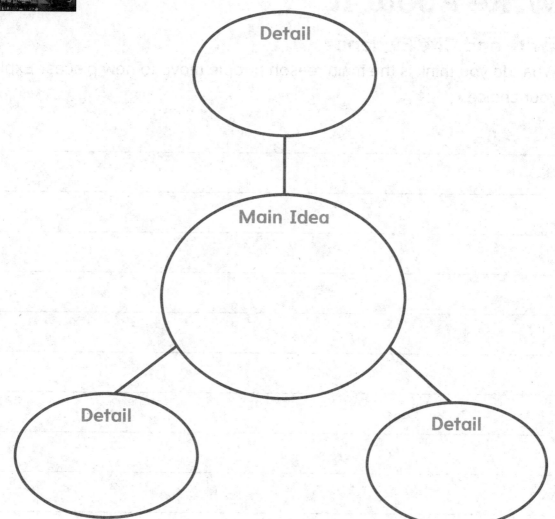

Detail

Main Idea

Detail

Detail

Think About It

Gather Evidence

Based on your research, why do you think people migrate to a new place?

Write About It

Write and Cite Evidence

What do you think is the main reason people move to new places? Explain your choice.

_____

_____

_____

_____

_____

_____

_____

_____

_____

_____

_____

_____

Talk About It

COLLABORATE

Explain

Compare your choice with the choice of a classmate. Take turns explaining your choices. Discuss why people often have several reasons for moving.

Geography

Connect to the

ESSENTIAL EQ QUESTION

Pull It Together

What are some ways that a community has changed over the years? What causes communities to change over time?

_____

_____

_____

_____

ESSENTIAL EQ QUESTION

Inquiry Project Notes

_____

_____

_____

_____

_____

_____

How Did Settlers and California Indians Interact?

Lesson Outcomes

What Am I Learning?

In this lesson, you will use your investigative skills to find out how European and American **settlers** lived with California Indians.

Why Am I Learning It?

Reading and talking about how California was settled will help you understand what happened to California Indian communities over time.

How Will I Know That I Learned It?

You will be able to tell about the changes that happen when different cultures meet.

Talk About It

COLLABORATE

Look closely at the picture. Who are the people? What are they doing? What do you think they see?

HSS.3.3.1, HSS.3.3.3, HAS.CS.1, HAS.HR.2

Explorers come to California shores.

1 Inspect

Read the first paragraph. What do you think the text will be about? Then read the article.

- **Circle** words you don't know.
- **Underline** what the Spanish and Americans expected of the California Indians.
- **Discuss** with a partner how the Spanish and Americans were similar to each other.

My Notes

_____

_____

_____

_____

_____

_____

A Clash of Cultures

American Indians were the first people to live in what is now California. They had lived in the area for thousands of years. They had similar beliefs and ways of life. European and American settlers who came to California brought their own cultures with them. Often, these cultures and ways of life were very different from how California Indians lived.

The Spanish arrived in California in the 1500s. They claimed California for their king. In the 1700s, they built presidios (forts) and missions on the land they claimed. A mission was a community of people living and working together. The mission was centered around a church. The Spanish expected the Indians to live on the mission. They expected them to change their religion. They expected them to give up their way of life.

Curtis (Edward S.) Collection, Library of Congress, LC-USZ62-110505

Students pose for a photo at an early California Indian reservation school.

In the 1800s, the United States gained control of California. American settlers moved into the region. Like the Spanish, they took the best land for themselves. They made the California Indians move from their homelands. The U.S. government made the Indians live on small reservations.

Like the Spanish, the Americans felt their culture was the only way of life. They expected the California Indians to live as Americans. They expected them to speak and dress like Americans. California Indians lost much of their culture during this time in the state's history.

2 Find Evidence

Reread How did the Spanish and Americans treat the California Indians? What information from the text supports your ideas?

Look at the photograph. How does it help you understand how the lives of California Indians changed?

3 Make Connections

Talk What happened to the California Indians? Discuss your answer with a partner.

COLLABORATE

Connect to Now Who lives in your community? Where are their ancestors from?

Explore Chronology

Identifying the **chronology**, or the order in which events occur, will help you understand how events in history are connected.

1. **Read the text once all the way through.**
   This will help you understand what the text is about.

2. **Look at the section titles to see how the text is organized.**
   Titles may offer clues as to which important events are discussed.

3. **Watch for specific dates.**
   Are the events presented in chronological order? It may help to look for sentences that begin with a date. Note that dates could be specific, such as "In 1492." They could also express a range of time, such as "In the 1800s."

4. **Find key facts about the events.**
   While reading, ask yourself what key facts are most important to remember about the settlement of California.

 COLLABORATE Based on the text you read, work with your class to complete the chart below.

Time Period	Key Facts
1500s	
1700s	
1800s	

Investigate!

Read pages 120–127 in your Research Companion. Use your investigative skills to look for text evidence that tells you when and what happened. This chart will help you organize your notes.

Time Period	Key Facts
1500s	
1600s	
1700s	
1800s	

Think About It

Gather Evidence

Review your research. Based on the information you have gathered, how did the lives of California Indians change with the arrival of newcomers?

Write About It

Write and Cite Evidence

In your opinion, what are some positive things that happen when different cultures meet? What are some negative things?

Talk About It

Defend Your Claim

Take turns discussing your responses with a classmate. Do you think the meeting of cultures in early California was more positive or negative?

History

Connect to the

Pull It Together

Think about the people and events that you read and talked about in this lesson. How did they change things for California today?

_____

_____

_____

_____

Inquiry Project Notes

_____

_____

_____

_____

_____

_____

How Do Communities of the Past Compare to Today?

Lesson Outcomes

What Am I Learning?

In this lesson, you will use your investigative skills to find out how a community changes over time.

Why Am I Learning It?

Reading and talking about what life was like in the past will help you learn how a community can change.

How Will I Know That I Learned It?

You will write a paragraph about life in the past and explain how life is different today. You also will give reasons why communities change and grow.

Talk About It

Look closely at the photos. Describe the buildings. Do they look like the buildings you see in your community today? Do they seem old or modern?

KazPhotography/iStock/Getty Images

How the Past Can Be Seen Today

1 Inspect

Read Look at the title. What do you think this text will be about?

- **Highlight** the names of two cities that show Spanish influence on California.
- **Underline** words that describe the various ethnic groups that live in California.
- **Discuss** with a partner what you think your community was like in the past.

My Notes

_____

_____

_____

_____

_____

_____

_____

_____

Read the names of these California cities: Santa Clarita and San Luis Obispo. The names are Spanish. This is because the Spanish formed these communities. The names help you understand the history of these cities. You can also learn about a community's history by looking at its buildings. The way a building looks can tell you who built it and when it was built. Buildings with red clay tile roofs and thick white walls are built in a Spanish style.

The population of California is diverse. Each community is made up of people from many different **ethnic groups** and backgrounds. The California Indians have lived here for thousands of years. Other groups of people came more recently. The first Spanish **settlers** came in the late 1700s, more than two hundred years ago. In the 1800s, people from Germany, Ireland, and China traveled to California looking for gold and good soil. Today, people from all over the world make California home.

People from many ethnic groups have affected your community. The signs you see or even the house you live in can show your community's history. You may eat foods from different cultures. You may celebrate the holidays of other cultures. The people who lived in your community in the past helped make your community what it is like today.

Crowds of people enjoy Grant Avenue in Chinatown, San Francisco.

2 Find Evidence

Reread What features of a community today tell you about the cultures and people of its past?

- **Underline** examples in the text of ethnic groups.

3 Make Connections

Talk What parts of your community remind you of the people who lived there long ago? How do these parts affect the people who live there now?

COLLABORATE

Explore Compare and Contrast

To **compare** is to tell how things are alike. To **contrast** is to tell how things are different. Your social studies text will sometimes compare and contrast two things or two time periods.

1. **Read the text once all the way through.**
   This will help you understand what the text is about.

2. **Look for words that signal a comparison or a contrast.**
   The text may use words such as *like, the same,* and *both* to compare two things. It may use words such as *unlike* and *different* to contrast two things.

3. **Now look for the big ideas that are being compared.**
   A text may compare and contrast two groups of people, two forms of transportation, or two time periods. Look for key words such as *in the past* and *in the present*.

4. **Ask: *How are these the same? How are they different?***
   Make a list or take notes on what is being compared.

 Based on the text you read, work with your class to complete the diagram below.

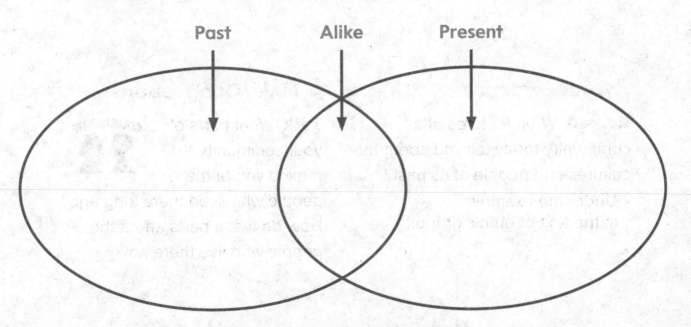

Past   Alike   Present

Investigate!

Read pages 128–137 in your Research Companion. Use your investigative skills to look for text evidence that tells you how things in the past and today are similar and different. This chart will help you organize your notes.

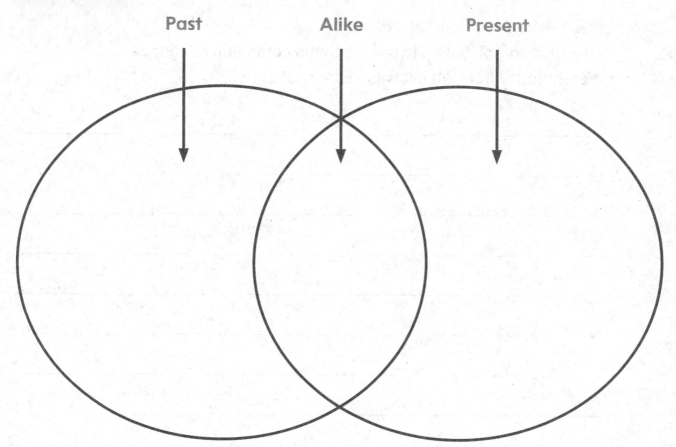

Past   Alike   Present

Think About It

Gather Evidence

What causes communities to change over time?

Write About It

Write and Cite Evidence

Write a paragraph telling two ways that a community might be different today from what it was in the past.

_____

_____

_____

_____

_____

_____

_____

_____

_____

_____

_____

_____

Talk About It

Contrast

Share your paragraph with a partner. Then talk about how your
community is different than it was a century ago.

 # Connect to the

Pull It Together

Think about the changes you have read and talked about in this lesson.
Which change do you think had the biggest impact on your community?

_____

_____

_____

_____

_____

 Inquiry Project Notes

_____

_____

_____

_____

_____

_____

_____

How Have People Changed the Land?

Lesson Outcomes

What Am I Learning?

In this lesson, you will use your investigative skills to find out why people change the land and how these changes affect the environment.

Why Am I Learning It?

Reading and talking about how people have changed the land will help you understand the difficulty of protecting the environment and meeting people's needs at the same time.

How Will I Know That I Learned It?

You will be able to explain two reasons why people change the environment and tell what effects those changes have had.

Talk About It

COLLABORATE

Look at the photographs. The smaller one shows a dam. The larger one shows the water behind the dam. How do you think the dam has changed the river and the land around it?

lightphoto/iStock/Getty Images

O'Shaughnessy Dam and Hetch Hetchy Reservoir in Yosemite National Park

Changing Our Landscape

1 Inspect

Read Underline the key ideas in the text.

- **Highlight** the details that tell how water can come to you from hundreds of miles away.

My Notes

_____

_____

_____

_____

_____

_____

_____

_____

_____

_____

_____

People change the land to meet their needs. Think about how you get to school. You probably take a bus that travels on roads for several miles. You may walk on a sidewalk along a street. Roads and sidewalks are changes people have made to the land to travel safely from place to place. We need to get from one place to another, so we build roads. We need food and water, so we change the land to get them. But making changes to the land to meet our needs can harm our environment.

We get water when we turn on the faucet. But where does the water come from? For many people in California, water comes from hundreds of miles away. To get water to you, people have had to change the land. They built dams to create reservoirs to gather and hold water. They built **aqueducts** (AK wuh dukts) from these dams to bring the water to your community. Now when people turn on a faucet, they can get water.

People have changed the land to bring water to homes.

2 Find Evidence

Reread What are the effects to the environment of building a dam?

3 Make Connections

Talk Discuss with a partner the positive and negative effects of building a dam.

COLLABORATE

How does bringing water to you affect the environment? A dam stops a river from flowing freely. A river has been blocked, so the area below the dam becomes drier. Fewer plants can grow because the land is dry. Animals have to go somewhere else to find food and water. The area above the dam is changed, too. There might have been a valley in the area behind the dam. This is now a deep lake. We changed the landscape to meet our need for water. In doing so, we greatly changed the environment of an entire region.

Michael Bodmann/E+/Getty Images

Explore Cause and Effect

An **effect** is what happened. A **cause** is why it happened. As you read, look out for something that causes another thing to happen.

1. **Read the text once all the way through.**
   This will help you understand what the text is about.

2. **Understand how causes and effects are related.**
   A cause happens before an effect. While you read, look for clue words that tell the order in which the events happened. Sometimes a cause may have many effects.

3. **Watch out for words that signal a cause or effect.**
   Words such as *since, because,* and *as a result* often indicate a cause-and-effect relationship.

4. **Ask yourself: *What happened? Why did it happen?***
   The answer to *Why did it happen?* is a cause.

 COLLABORATE Based on the text you read, work with your class to complete the chart below.

Cause	Effect
People need to travel from one place to another.	
	People build dams.
People build dams.	

Investigate!

Read pages 138–145 in your Research Companion. Use your investigative skills to look for text evidence that tells you what happened and why it happened. This chart will help you organize your notes.

Cause	Effect
	People make tunnels or flatten mountains to build roads.
Food cannot grow in the desert.	
Water is carried to cities and farms.	
More people move to California.	
	Air pollution

Think About It

Gather Evidence

Review your research. Based on the information you have gathered, what causes people to change the land?

Write About It

Write and Cite Evidence

Write a paragraph explaining two reasons why people change the land. What effects have these changes had on the land?

_____

_____

_____

_____

_____

_____

_____

_____

_____

_____

_____

Talk About It

Defend Your Claim

Work in small groups. Take turns discussing your paragraphs. What examples did your classmates use? Explain why some changes to the land can be good and why some can be bad.

Geography

Connect to the

Pull It Together

Think about what you have read and talked about in this lesson. How have changes to the land affected your community?

_____

_____

_____

_____

Inquiry Project Notes

_____

_____

_____

_____

_____

_____

_____

How Do Communities Develop?

Lesson Outcomes

What Am I Learning?

In this lesson, you will use your investigative skills to find out how a community has become what it is today.

Why Am I Learning It?

Reading and talking about the history of your community helps you understand how your community works today.

How Will I Know That I Learned It?

You will be able to create a list of features in your community that you want to learn more about. Then you will name features in your community that would attract newcomers.

Talk About It

COLLABORATE

Look closely at the picture on the next page. Why do you think the city of San Diego has a monument to a European explorer?

Ron Thomas/E+/Getty Images

Cabrillo National Monument on Point Loma Peninsula in San Diego

vivalapenler/iStock/Getty Images

Using the Local News

News sources are one way for you to learn about your community's history. They also help you learn about your community today. It is important for citizens to know what is going on in their communities. Newspapers, websites, and television stations are just some of the ways people can get the news.

Many large cities have newspapers and websites that are read across the country. The *Los Angeles Times* is an example of a big city newspaper that is read by people across the United States. It publishes articles about local, state, and national events every day to help keep people informed.

Smaller communities also have newspapers, websites, and blogs. The newspapers may be printed only once a week. However, websites and blogs are updated more often. Local news sources are important because people need to know what is going on in their communities.

What kinds of local news sources are available in your community? What kinds of information do they provide?

Papers tell us what is going on in our community and in our nation.

McGraw-Hill Education

2 Find Evidence

Reread Why would local citizens want to read a local news source?

Contrast How do you think information in newspapers, websites, or blogs from smaller communities is different from information in television news and newspapers from large cities?

3 Make Connections

Talk Discuss with your classmates the different ways you can find local news. How can local news help you learn about your community?

COLLABORATE

Explore Summarizing

How do you tell a friend about a local event that you read or heard about? You tell about the event using your own words. This is what you do when you summarize. In a summary, you tell the important details of what you read in your own words.

1. **Read the text once all the way through.**
   This will help you understand the topic.

2. **Look for the main idea of each section.**
   If there are subheadings, these give clues to the main idea.

3. **Look for key details.**
   Details tell more about the main idea.

4. **Retell the information in your own words.**
   Include the main ideas and the most important details.

 COLLABORATE Based on the text you read, work with your class to complete the chart below.

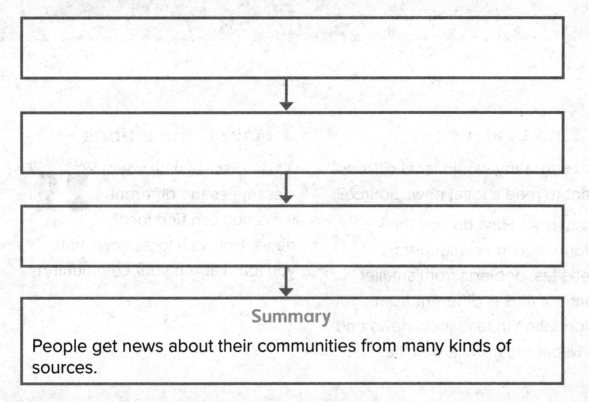

Summary

People get news about their communities from many kinds of sources.

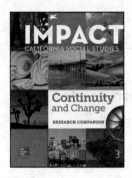

Investigate!

Read pages 146–153 in your Research Companion. Use your investigative skills to summarize the information about Santa Clara. This chart will help you organize your notes.

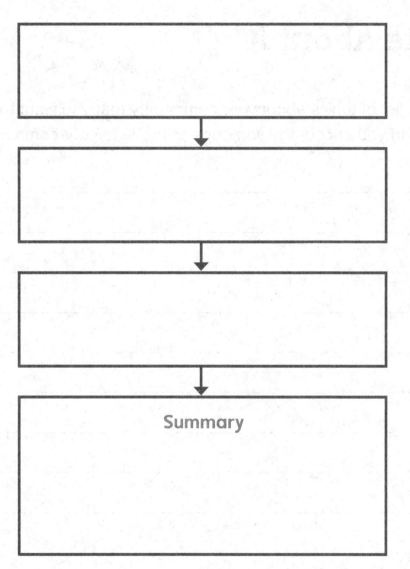

Summary

Think About It

Gather Information

Based on your research on Santa Clara, what information do you want to find out about your community? What resources could you use to learn about your community and its history?

Write About It

Explain

Create a list of topics about your community that you want to research. How could you encourage someone to move to your community?

_____

_____

_____

_____

_____

_____

_____

_____

_____

_____

_____

_____

Talk About It

Explain

Compare your lists with a classmate. Pick features from both lists that you think would encourage people to move to your community.

 History
Connect to the

Pull It Together

Think about the ways your community has changed over the years. How have these changes affected the lives of people living in the community today?

_____

_____

_____

_____

_____

_____

_____

Inquiry Project Notes

_____

_____

_____

Lesson Outcomes

What Am I Learning?

In this lesson, you will use your investigative
skills to find out how communities are special.

Why Am I Learning It?

Reading and talking about why a community is special
will help you learn how geography, history,
and cultures affect the people who live in
a community.

How Will I Know That I
Learned It?

You will be able to tell what makes a
community special. You will be able
to write about your own community
and describe what makes it special.

Talk About It COLLABORATE

Look closely at the photograph on the
next page. What details in it do you find
interesting? What do you think it shows
about communities in California?

California Indian dancers perform the Blessing of the Animals at a festival in Los Angeles.

Edward Vasquez/Alamy Stock Photo

Linking to the Past

One thing that can make a community special is its past. As communities grow and change, it is important to remember the past.

San Francisco has changed greatly over the years. The Ohlone Indians lived in the area before the Spanish arrived. After the Spanish came, they built the Presidio and Mission Dolores in 1774. In time, San Francisco became one of California's largest and most important cities. During the Gold Rush of 1849, the city grew quickly. In 1906, it survived a major earthquake and fires. Through all of this, San Francisco has kept links to its rich and interesting past. Let's look at one of those links.

The "Painted Ladies" Victorian houses in San Francisco survived the 1906 earthquake.

Jim Boud/Flickr RF/Getty Images

A cable car runs on California Street in San Francisco.

San Francisco's cable cars are famous around the world. Andrew Hallidie invented the cable car in 1873 after he saw a horse-drawn cart fall down a steep hill. He designed a car that could be pulled up and down the hills by cables in the street. The cable helps control the car when it goes downhill. The cable cars were a big success.

In the 1940s, cable cars began to seem old-fashioned. The mayor of San Francisco planned to get rid of them. However, the people of San Francisco fought hard to keep the cars. They were part of the city's history. The people won. Today, the cable cars are an important tourist attraction and part of what makes San Francisco a special place.

2 Find Evidence

Reread Why were cable cars safer than a horse and cart?

Underline clues that support your ideas.

3 Make Connections

Talk Discuss with a partner why he or she thinks cable cars are an important part of San Francisco's history. What do you know about your community's history? What things from the past do you still find in your town?

COLLABORATE

Explore Drawing Conclusions

A **conclusion** is a decision you make about a topic. You use what you already know and information from what you are reading to draw a conclusion.

1. **Read the text.**
   Think about how the details and ideas in the text are connected.

2. **Think about what you already know about this topic.**
   Sometimes the author does not tell you everything. You have to use what you already know to understand the text.

3. **Draw a conclusion.**
   Draw a conclusion using what you read and what you know.

COLLABORATE Based on the text you read, work with your class to complete the chart below to answer the question: "How do the people of San Francisco feel about the cable cars?"

Clues and What I Already Know	Conclusions

Investigate!

Read pages 154–161 in your Research Companion. Use your investigative skills to look for text evidence that tells you why communities are special. Then draw conclusions about what makes a community a special place. This chart will help you organize your notes.

Text Clues and What I Already Know About Communities	Conclusions

Think About It

Review

Recall what you have learned through your research. Why do you think all communities are different?

Write About It

Define

What things can make a community special?

_____

_____

_____

_____

_____

In Your Opinion

Write a blog post about your community, its people, and its places. List reasons why you think your community is special.

_____

_____

_____

_____

_____

Talk About It

Compare and Contrast

Share your blog post with a classmate. Compare and contrast your ideas. Then brainstorm additional reasons your community is special. Why is it one of a kind?

History

Connect to the

Pull It Together

Think about the role history has played in making your community special. How have events and people of the past affected your community?

_____

_____

_____

_____

 Inquiry Project Notes

_____

_____

_____

_____

_____

_____

Step Back in Time

CHARACTERS

Narrator	**Teacher**
Tour Guide	**Maria** *a girl from 1910*
Maya *a girl from the present day*	**Maria's little sisters and brothers**
Binh *a boy from the present day*	*(non-speaking parts)*
	Joe *Maria's brother*

Narrator: Maya and Binh are in the third grade. They are on a class trip. They are visiting a museum to learn about immigrants who came to their community long ago. To their surprise, they find an unexpected exhibit.

Tour Guide: Welcome to the museum. Today we will learn what life was like for people who came to the United States long ago. Let's start by seeing the kind of place where many immigrants lived.

(Maya, Binh, and the Teacher follow the Tour Guide.)

Tour Guide: More than one hundred years ago, an immigrant family lived in an apartment like this. Ten people might have slept in this one room.

Maya: And I thought my apartment was crowded!

Tour Guide: Please follow me to the next room.

(The Tour Guide leaves. The Teacher follows. Maya turns to leave, but Binh stops her.)

Binh: Look, Maya. A door! Let's take a look.

Narrator: This was no ordinary door. This door belonged to a time machine.

(Binh opens the door, and Maya follows him. Maria, a 10-year-old girl from 1910, is cooking over a stove. Smaller children surround her.)

Maria: Hello. Are you here to rent the apartment upstairs?

Maya: I don't think so.

Maria: Then why are you here?

Binh: We're here on a school trip.

Maria: School? Don't you have to work?

Maya: No. We're only eight.

Maria: Well, I'm 10. I've had a job since I was five.

Binh: What kind of work do you do?

Maria: I help my mother make clothes. She sells them. *(Pause)* What strange clothes you are wearing. We do not wear such things in 1910.

Maya: *(to Binh)* Did she say 1910? What does she mean?

Binh: *(to Maya)* We must have traveled back in time!

Maria: Where are you from?

Binh: I was born in Vietnam.

Maya: I'm from California.

Maria: I was born in Italy. It's hard moving to a new country, isn't it? Do you miss your homeland?

Binh: Yes, I miss my grandparents. They still live in Vietnam.

Maria: I miss my grandparents, too! I visited them every day when I lived in Italy.

Binh: I did, too, in Vietnam.

Maria: Now, I'll never see them again.

Maya: Can't you take an airplane and fly back to see them?

Maria: Airplane? Fly? What are you talking about? I'd have to take a boat to go back to Italy. Besides, it costs too much money.

Binh: Do you like it in the United States?

Maria: Yes, I like a lot of things about the United States. People come here from all over the world.

Maya: I like that about the United States, too.

Maria: But it was hard to learn to speak English. My brother Joe taught me. He goes to school during the day. He works at night lighting the street lamps. Oh, I hear him walking up the stairs now.

(Joe enters. He carries books under his arm.)

Joe: Hello, Maria. Who are these people?

Maria: Joe, these are my new friends. *(to Binh)* Don't worry about missing your homeland. Life will get better, I promise.

(Maria and Joe say "goodbye" as Binh and Maya exit through the door.)

Maya: Wow! Life was very different in 1910!

Binh: Can you imagine going to school and working?

(The Teacher walks in.)

Teacher: *(smiling)* There you are! I hope you saw something interesting.

Binh/Maya: *(speaking together)* We sure did!

Talk About It

COLLABORATE

With a partner, discuss what your first day at school might be like if you moved to a different country.

Inquiry Project Wrap-Up

Sequencing Your Community's Development

Now is the time for your team to share your timeline with the rest of the class. Here's what to do.

- ☐ Have each team member prepare to tell about a part of the timeline.

- ☐ Show your timeline to the class. Imagine that you are giving visitors a tour of your community.

- ☐ Explain how these events and locations affected the growth of your community.

- ☐ Share with the class how your team chose which events and locations to include in the timeline.

Tips for Presenting

Remember these tips when you present to the class.

- ☐ Prepare for the presentation.

- ☐ Make sure what you say is based on fact.

- ☐ Speak clearly and use complete sentences.

- ☐ Relax and enjoy yourself!

Project Rubric

Use these questions to help evaluate your project.

	Yes	No
Did your team select events that helped your community grow?		
Did you write clear descriptions of the events?		
Did your team identify locations that represent the key events?		
Did every team member prepare to present a part of the timeline?		
Were you happy with the timeline your team created?		

Project Reflection

Think about the work that you did in this chapter with a group.
Describe how well you worked with the other members of your group.
What could you have done to help the group work better together?

_____

_____

_____

_____

Chapter 4

American Citizens, Symbols, and Government

How Do Our Government and Its Citizens Work Together?

In this chapter, you will learn how our governments are organized and how they work. You will learn about citizenship. You will also explore what it means to be a good citizen. With your class, you will work on a chapter project to write a constitution that sets classroom rules.

COLLABORATE

Talk About It

Discuss with a partner the questions you have about government and being a good citizen.

My Research Questions

1. _____

_____

2. _____

_____

 **Inquiry Project**

Creating a Classroom Constitution

In this project, you will work with your class to create a classroom constitution that sets the rules everyone must follow to make your classroom a fair and safe community.

Here's your project checklist.

☐ **Set** a purpose for your classroom constitution.

☐ **Think** about how you should behave in the classroom.

☐ **List** a set of rules that everyone must follow.

☐ **Discuss** the consequences for breaking a rule.

☐ **Write** a constitution that describes rules for your class and the consequences for breaking a rule.

☐ **Agree** to follow the constitution.

Explore / Words

Complete this chapter's Word Rater. Write notes as you learn more about each word.

amendment
My Notes

☐ Know It!

☐ Heard It! _____

☐ Don't Know It! _____

_____

citizen
My Notes

☐ Know It! _____

☐ Heard It! _____

☐ Don't Know It! _____

_____

compromise
My Notes

☐ Know It! _____

☐ Heard It! _____

☐ Don't Know It! _____

_____

executive branch
My Notes

☐ Know It! _____

☐ Heard It! _____

☐ Don't Know It! _____

_____

federal
My Notes

☐ Know It! _____

☐ Heard It! _____

☐ Don't Know It! _____

_____

judicial branch

My Notes

☐ Know It!

☐ Heard It!

☐ Don't Know It!

_____

_____

_____

jury

My Notes

☐ Know It!

☐ Heard It!

☐ Don't Know It!

_____

_____

_____

legislative branch

My Notes

☐ Know It!

☐ Heard It!

☐ Don't Know It!

_____

_____

_____

right

My Notes

☐ Know It!

☐ Heard It!

☐ Don't Know It!

_____

_____

_____

tax

My Notes

☐ Know It!

☐ Heard It!

☐ Don't Know It!

_____

_____

Lesson Outcomes

What Am I Learning?

In this lesson, you will use your investigative skills to find out about the United States Constitution.

Why Am I Learning It?

Reading and talking about the Constitution will help you understand how our government is set up.

How Will I Know That I Learned It?

You will be able to write a list of items that might be in a classroom constitution.

The U.S. Constitution

Talk About It COLLABORATE

Look closely at the picture on the next page. What do you think the room was used for? Why do you think so?

Fotosearch/Fotosearch RF/Getty Images

HSS.3.4.1, HSS.3.4.3, HAS.HR.2

180 Lesson 1   Why Is the Constitution of the United States Important?

The Assembly Room in Independence Hall, Philadelphia, Pennsylvania

Preamble of the United States Constitution

1 Inspect

Read the first paragraph. What is a preamble?

- **Circle** any words in the preamble that you do not know.
- **Underline** the words that tell *who* the Constitution is written for.
- **Discuss** with a partner the reasons *why* the Constitution was written. Then restate one of the reasons in your own words.

My Notes

_____

_____

_____

_____

_____

_____

_____

Have you ever heard or seen the words "We the People"? You can find them at the beginning of our nation's Constitution. This part is called the preamble. The preamble introduces the Constitution. The opening words show that the United States government is run by its people and for its people. The preamble also lists the reasons why the Constitution was written. Let's read the preamble to find out more!

> **PRIMARY SOURCE**

"We the People of the United States, in Order to form a more perfect Union, establish Justice, insure domestic Tranquility, provide for the common defence, promote the general Welfare, and secure the Blessings of Liberty to ourselves and our Posterity, do ordain and establish this Constitution for the United States of America."

—Preamble to the United States Constitution

The Constitution of the United States begins with the words "We the People."

The preamble also tells about American beliefs. For example, the people of the United States are very important. The government gets its power from the people. Also, it is important for the states to join together. They are stronger as one country.

2 Find Evidence

Reread the preamble. How many reasons are listed for why the Constitution was written? Why do you think the founders listed so many reasons?

Think about the phrase "promote the general Welfare." What does the word *welfare* mean? Name a word that has a similar meaning.

3 Make Connections

Talk Discuss with a partner the reasons why the Constitution was written. Which do you think is most important? Why?

COLLABORATE

Explore Main Idea and Details

The topic is what a text is about. The **main idea** is the most important idea of a topic. **Details** tell more about the main idea.

1. **Read the text once all the way through.**
   This will help you understand what the text is about.

2. **Use section titles to identify topics.**
   A section title often tells you the topic of that section.

3. **Ask yourself: *What is the most important idea about this topic?***
   The most important idea is the main idea of the text.

4. **Look for information that tells more about the main ideas.**
   These are details. They help you understand the main idea.

 COLLABORATE Based on the text you read, work with your class to complete the chart below.

Main Idea	Details
The preamble introduces the U.S. Constitution.	

Investigate!

Read pages 172–179 in your Research Companion. Use your investigative skills to look for details that tell more about the main ideas listed in the chart. This chart will help you organize your notes.

Main Ideas	Details
The Articles of Confederation were the first plan for the government of the United States.	
At the Constitutional Convention, a new constitution was written for the United States.	
The Constitution divides the U.S. government into three branches.	

Think About It

Take a Stand

Why might a constitution for your classroom be helpful?
Think about what might be contained in the constitution.

Write About It

Write a List of Ideas

Work with a partner to write a list of items that might be in
a classroom constitution.

_____

_____

_____

_____

_____

_____

_____

_____

_____

_____

_____

Talk About It

Compare and Contrast

Share your list with your classmates. Compare and contrast your ideas.
Then discuss which ideas are most important to include in a class constitution.

Citizenship

Connect to the

Pull It Together

How does the Constitution help our government and its citizens
to work together?

_____

_____

_____

_____

Inquiry Project Notes

_____

_____

_____

_____

_____

_____

How Do the Branches of Government Work Together?

Lesson Outcomes

What Am I Learning?

In this lesson, you will use your investigative skills to understand the branches of government.

Why Am I Learning It?

Reading and talking about how the government is set up will help you understand how it works.

How Will I Know That I Learned It?

You will be able to explain what each branch does and tell how they work together.

PHOTO: Prints and Photographs Division, Library of Congress, LC-USZ62-13026
TEXT: Meyers, Robert C. V. Theodore Roosevelt: Patriot and Statesman. Philadelphia, PA: P.W. Zieglar & Co., 1902.

PRIMARY SOURCE

In Their Words... President Roosevelt

"We get in the habit of speaking of the Government as if it were something apart from us. Now, the Government is us—we are the Government, you and I. And the Government is going to do well or ill accordingly as we make up our minds that the affairs of the Government shall be managed."

—Speech by President Theodore Roosevelt given in Asheville, North Carolina, 1902, as recorded by Robert C. V. Meyers

HAS.CS.2

Edwin Remsberg/Alamy Stock Photo

People going to work in Washington, D.C.

Talk About It

COLLABORATE

Read the Primary Source quote. What does President Roosevelt mean by saying "we are the Government"?

Working for the Future

1 Inspect

Read President Obama's speech. What is he speaking about?

- **Underline** the words you think are the most important in the speech.
- **Discuss** with a partner what President Obama thinks American citizens should do.

My Notes

_____

_____

_____

_____

_____

_____

_____

_____

Every year the President of the United States gives a speech called the State of the Union to the American people. Read what President Obama said in his 2016 State of the Union address.

PRIMARY SOURCE

In Their Words... President Barack Obama

"We the People." Our Constitution begins with those three simple words, words we've come to recognize mean all the people, not just some; words that insist we rise and fall together....

The future we want—all of us want—opportunity and security for our families, a rising standard of living, a sustainable, peaceful planet for our kids—all that is within our reach. But it will only happen if we work together....

So, my fellow Americans... our collective future depends on your willingness to uphold your duties as a citizen. To vote. To speak out. To stand up for others, especially the weak, especially the vulnerable, knowing that each of us is only here because somebody, somewhere, stood up for us.

TEXT: Obama, Barack. "Remarks of President Barack Obama - State of the Union Address As Delivered." State of the Union, Washington, D.C., January 13, 2016.

President Barack Obama delivers the State of the Union address in 2014.

2 Find Evidence

Examine Read the statement, "To stand up for others, especially the weak, especially the vulnerable, knowing that each of us is only here because somebody, somewhere, stood up for us." What does it mean to "stand up for" other people? Name a word that has the same meaning as "stand up for."

3 Make Connections

Talk Discuss with a partner why working together is important.

COLLABORATE

Connect to Now What are some ways you can work together in your classroom or community?

Explore Main Idea and Details

The **main idea** is the most important point the author makes about a topic. Key **details** tell about the main idea.

1. **Read the text once all the way through.**
   This will help you understand what the text is about.

2. **Reread the text and look for the most important idea.**
   This is the main idea.

3. **Look for an idea or example that tells about the main idea.**
   This is a detail.

4. **Look for another detail that tells about the main idea.**
   How many details can you find?

 COLLABORATE Work with your class to complete the chart below, using details from President Obama's speech.

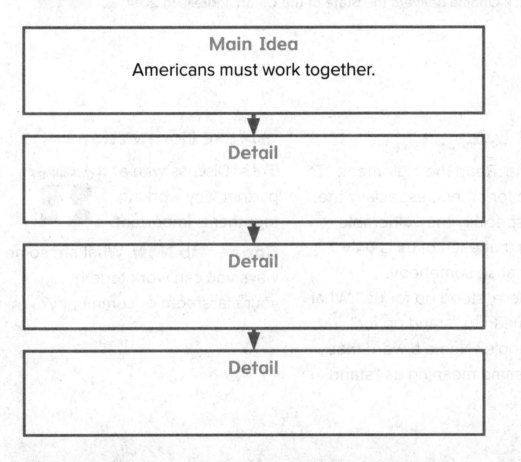

Main Idea
Americans must work together.

↓

Detail

↓

Detail

↓

Detail

Investigate!

Read pages 180–189 in your Research Companion. Use your investigative skills to find details that tell about the main idea. This chart will help you organize your notes.

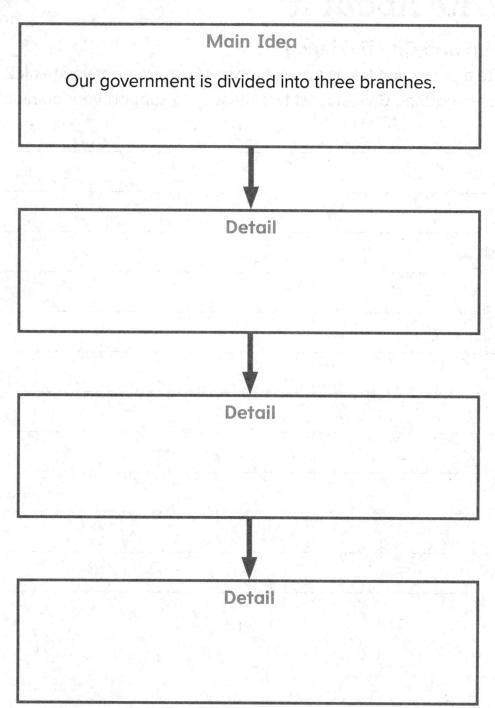

Main Idea

Our government is divided into three branches.

↓

Detail

↓

Detail

↓

Detail

Think About It

Interpret

Based on your research, how do you think the three branches of U.S. government work together?

Write About It

Write and Cite Evidence

Write a paragraph telling which branch of government you think is the most important. Give at least two reasons to support your opinion.

_____

_____

_____

_____

_____

_____

_____

_____

_____

Talk About It

Defend Your Claim

Share your writing with a partner who wrote about a different branch of government. Take turns talking about your opinions. Do you agree or disagree with your partner's opinion? Why?

Civics

Connect to the

Pull It Together

In what ways do you think the branches of government can do a better job of working together? How can you help?

1. _____

2. _____

3. _____

Inquiry Project Notes

_____

_____

_____

_____

_____

_____

Why Do Communities Need Governments?

Lesson Outcomes

What Am I Learning?

In this lesson, you will use your investigative skills to learn about the governments in California.

Why Am I Learning It?

Reading and talking about the governments in California will help you understand why communities need governments.

How Will I Know That I Learned It?

You will be able to write a blog post about your local government and how it serves your community.

Talk About It

COLLABORATE

Look at the photograph and read the caption on the next page. Which branch of the California government is shown here? Why do you think so?

HSS.3.4.4, HSS.3.4.5

CONNIE CONWAY

A discussion by lawmakers at the State Capitol in Sacramento

TEXT: Marshall, John. "U.S. Supreme Court: Worchester v. Georgia, 31 U.S. 6 Pet. 515 (1832)." United States Supreme Court, 1832.

1 Inspect

Read the Primary Source quote. Who wrote this?

- **Circle** the subject of the page.
- **Underline** the main thing John Marshall said about Indian nations.

My Notes

_____

_____

_____

_____

_____

_____

A Supreme Court Ruling

The Cherokee Indians lived in the southeastern United States. In the early 1800s, leaders in the state of Georgia tried to make the Cherokee people move from their homelands. Samuel Worcester, a friend of the Cherokee, lived on their land. Leaders in Georgia did not want Worcester to help the Cherokee. They passed a law saying that only Cherokee Indians could live on Cherokee land. Worcester was arrested for breaking this law. He was sent to prison.

Worcester asked the Supreme Court to hear his case. In 1832, the Supreme Court ruled the Georgia law was wrong. John Marshall was the Chief Justice of the Supreme Court. He wrote

PRIMARY SOURCE

In Their Words... Chief Justice John Marshall

"Indian Nations have always been considered as distinct, independent political communities, retaining their original natural rights, as the undisputed possessors of the soil.... The very term 'nation' so generally applied to them, means 'a people distinct from others.'"

—United States Supreme Court, 1832

that American Indian nations are separate and independent from the United States. Justice Marshall said that states could not tell an Indian nation what to do. It was an important decision.

Yurok Tribe Executive Director Troy Fletcher talking with state officials about the Klamath River land.

2 Find Evidence

Reread the statement "Indian Nations have always been considered as distinct, independent political communities." What does the word *independent* mean? Name a word that has the same meaning as *independent*.

3 Make Connections

Talk Summarize John Marshall's comments in your own words.

COLLABORATE

Explore Summarizing

A **summary** is a short retelling of the important ideas of a text. You summarize main ideas and key ideas.

1. **Read the text once all the way through.**

2. **Look for the main ideas.**
   Authors often state the main ideas at the beginning or the end of a paragraph.

3. **Reread the text and look for key details.**
   These are the details that support the main idea.

4. **Tell what the text says in your own words.**
   Include main ideas and key details. A summary uses fewer words than the text.

 COLLABORATE Based on the text you read, work with your class to complete the chart.

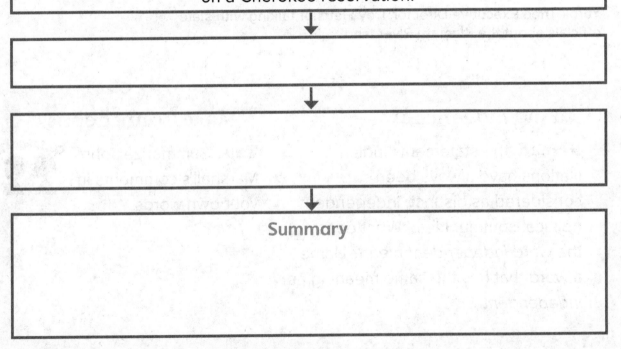

Leaders in Georgia arrested a non-Cherokee man living on a Cherokee reservation.

↓

↓

↓

Summary

Investigate!

Read pages 190–199 in your Research Companion. Use your investigative skills to look for the most important ideas to include in a summary. This chart will help you organize your notes.

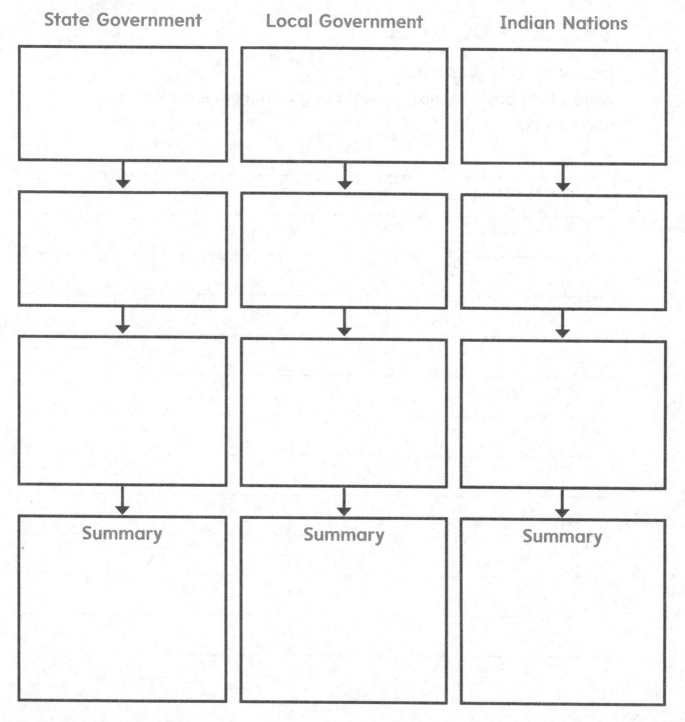

State Government	Local Government	Indian Nations
↓	↓	↓
↓	↓	↓
↓	↓	↓
Summary	Summary	Summary

Think About It

Contrast

Review your research on local government. How is it different from state and national governments? What kinds of services do local governments provide?

Write About It

Describe and Explain

Write a blog post describing your local government and explaining how it works.

_____

_____

_____

_____

_____

_____

_____

_____

_____

_____

_____

Talk About It

COLLABORATE

Explain

Share your blog post with a partner. Discuss the services local government provides in your community.

Civics

Connect to the

ESSENTIAL EQ QUESTION

Pull It Together

Do you think citizens could manage with only local governments? Give reasons for your answer.

_____

_____

_____

_____

_____

ESSENTIAL EQ QUESTION

Inquiry Project Notes

_____

_____

_____

_____

_____

_____

What Are Some Rules That We Must Follow?

Lesson Outcomes

What Am I Learning?
In this lesson, you will use your investigative skills to learn about the rules and laws we must follow each day.

Why Am I Learning It?
Reading and talking about rules and laws will help you understand how they keep people in your community safe.

How Will I Know That I Learned It?
You will be able to write about some rules you follow and tell why they are important.

EMPLOYEES MUST WASH HANDS!

EMPLOYEES ONLY

Talk About It

COLLABORATE

Look closely at the picture on the next page. What rules are being followed? Why are these rules needed in the community?

michaeldb/age fotostock

HSS.3.4.1, HSS.3.4.2

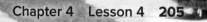

Anderson Ross/Alamy Stock Photo

Safety Rules and Laws

1 Inspect

Read the title and look at the photographs. What do you think this text will be about?

- **Circle** the word *fine*. What clues help you figure out what it means?
- **Underline** clues that tell you why sports have rules about wearing safety equipment.
- **Underline** what the punishment is for people who do not wear their seat belts.

My Notes

_____

_____

_____

_____

_____

_____

_____

Have you ever played football or soccer? These sports have rules the players must follow. In football, you must wear a helmet and pads to play. In soccer, you usually wear shin guards. Why do you think sports have these rules? The rules are to help keep the players safe.

The laws of your community also help keep you safe. Here's an example. People who wear seat belts are less likely to get hurt in a car accident. So California has made it a law that you must always wear a seat belt when riding in a car. If people do not wear one, they could get a ticket and pay a fine.

Seat belts keep us safe when we ride in a car.

Karen Town/E+/Getty Images

Car seats help keep babies safe and sound in a car.

Thousands of people are hurt in car accidents every year. The police started the *Click It or Ticket* program to protect people in cars. Laws help make sure every person in a car wears a seat belt. The police can stop a driver if they see someone in the car not wearing a seat belt. An adult can be fined $162. A parent can be fined $465 if a child is not buckled up! California takes car safety very seriously. You should too! Communities make rules and laws to keep people safe.

2 Find Evidence

Reread Why is it important to obey laws?

Examine What are the consequences of breaking seat belt laws?

3 Make Connections

Talk Why did California police start *Click It or Ticket*? Do you think this program will make people wear seat belts?

COLLABORATE

Roy Hsu/Blend Images/Getty Images

Explore Cause and Effect

A **cause** is why something happens. An **effect** is what happens. As you read, look for the causes of things.

1. **Read the text once all the way through.**
   This will help you understand what the text is about.

2. **Look for signal words such as *because* and *as a result*.**
   These clues often show a cause-and-effect relationship.

3. **Think about time order.**
   A cause happens before an effect.

4. **Ask *why* something happened. This reason is the cause.**

5. **Remember that a cause may have more than one effect.**

 COLLABORATE Based on the text you read, work with your class to complete the chart below.

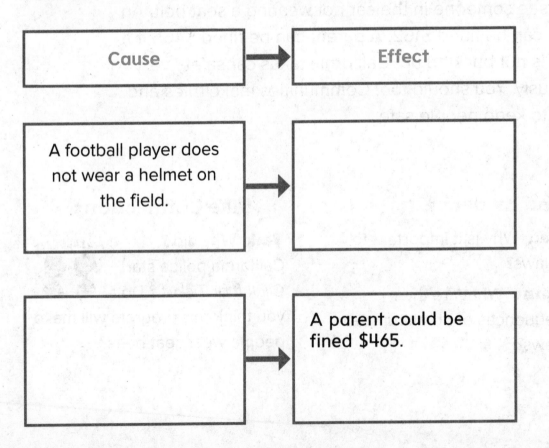

Cause	→	Effect
A football player does not wear a helmet on the field.	→	
	→	A parent could be fined $465.

Investigate!

Read pages 200–205 in your Research Companion. Use your investigative skills to look for text evidence that tells you what happened and why it happened. This chart will help you organize your notes.

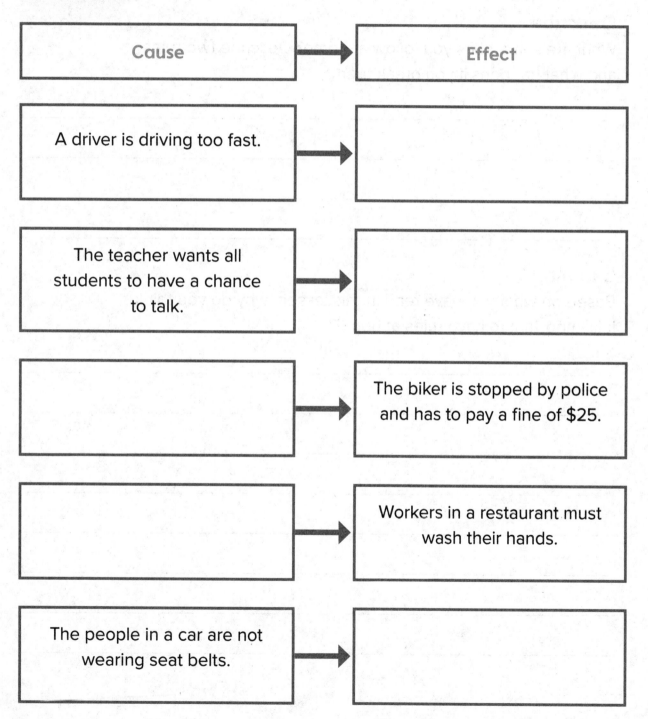

Cause	→	Effect
A driver is driving too fast.	→	
The teacher wants all students to have a chance to talk.	→	
	→	The biker is stopped by police and has to pay a fine of $25.
	→	Workers in a restaurant must wash their hands.
The people in a car are not wearing seat belts.	→	

Think About It

Ask Yourself

Why do you think it is important to have rules and laws?

Write About It

Describe

What are some rules you follow at home? Describe two rules and what happens if you break them.

_____

_____

_____

_____

Explain

Based on what you have read in this lesson, why do you think it is important to have rules at home?

_____

_____

_____

_____

_____

_____

_____

Talk About It

Discuss

Share your rules, their consequences, and the reasons for them with a partner. How are your rules similar to or different from your partner's rules?

Civics

Connect to the

Pull It Together

Think about what you read in this lesson. How do rules and laws help us all live together?

_____

_____

_____

_____

_____

 Inquiry Project Notes

_____

_____

_____

_____

_____

How Has Citizenship Changed Over Time?

Lesson Outcomes

What Am I Learning?

In this lesson, you will use your investigative skills to understand what it means to be a good **citizen** and how citizenship has changed in the United States over time.

Why Am I Learning It?

Reading and talking about the history of citizenship will help you understand how people affect their community and country.

How Will I Know That I Learned It?

You will be able to list the ways citizenship has changed over time in the United States and write about what it is like to be an American citizen today.

Talk About It

COLLABORATE

Look closely at the picture. What are the people doing? Why do you think this might be important?

Lisa J. Goodman/Moment Mobile/Getty Images

Timeline

1870
Non-white men and freed slaves gain the right to vote through passage of the 15th Amendment.

1971
Passage of the 26th Amendment lowers the voting age to 18.

1700 | | | | | | 1800 | | | | | | 1900 | | | | | | | 2000

1789
Only white men who are at least 21 years old and own land or pay taxes could vote.

1856
All white men are allowed to vote.

1920
Women gain the right to vote through passage of the 19th Amendment.

POLLING PLACE
投票站 CASILLA ELECTORAL
投票所 LUGAR NG BOTOHAN
투표소 PHÒNG PHIẾU

One way to practice good citizenship

Women Fight for Equality

1 Inspect

Read the title. What do you think this text will be about?

- **Circle** words you don't know.
- **Underline** clues that tell you why Susan B. Anthony was arrested.
- **Discuss** with a partner what citizens do when they vote.

My Notes

_____

_____

_____

_____

_____

_____

_____

_____

What makes a good citizen? Every citizen has a duty to be involved in the government. The **right** to vote enables each citizen to perform that duty. When we vote, we make decisions about which people we want to serve in the government. These are the people who make our laws.

The U.S. government did not always allow all citizens to vote. At first, women and African Americans did not have a constitutional right to vote. In the late 1800s, women came together to begin the fight for this right.

Susan B. Anthony helped lead this cause. She spoke to crowds of people and made sure the voices of women were heard. She was even arrested when she voted in an election before women had the right to vote. Susan B. Anthony died in 1906, before women won the right to vote. After her death, other women joined together to continue the fight.

PRIMARY SOURCE

In Their Words...
Susan B. Anthony

"Friends and fellow citizens: I stand before you tonight under indictment for the alleged crime of having voted at the last presidential election, without having a lawful right to vote. It shall be my work this evening to prove to you that in thus voting, I not only committed no crime, but, instead, simply exercised my citizen's rights, guaranteed to me and all United States citizens by the National Constitution, beyond the power of any state to deny."

—from a speech in 1873

2 Find Evidence

Reread the words from Susan B. Anthony's speech. Why do you think she gave this speech?

Examine the last sentence of the speech. What does "exercised my citizen's rights" mean?

3 Make Connections

Talk about how women fought for the right to vote. Was the fight successful?

COLLABORATE

   Women protested in front of the White House in Washington, D.C. They held marches in cities across the nation. They made sure the government knew they wanted to vote. In 1920, the government changed the Constitution when Congress passed the 19th Amendment. This guarantees voting rights for American women. Today, women use their right to vote to help decide how the government is run.

Explore Summarizing

When you **summarize**, you retell important ideas from a text. You retell these ideas in your own words. You should not copy the text directly.

1. **Read the text once all the way through.**
   This will help you understand what the text is about.

2. **Read the text again and look for the most important ideas.**
   Use your own words to state these important ideas.

3. **Put your words together to create a summary.**
   Write a paragraph retelling the most important ideas of the text.

COLLABORATE Based on the text you read, work with your class to identify the important ideas you can use to summarize how women got the right to vote.

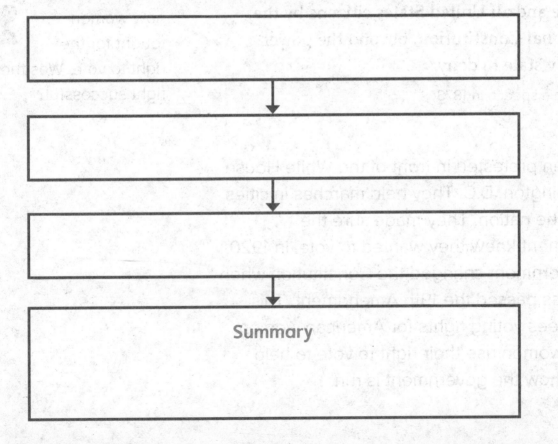

Summary

Investigate!

Read pages 206–215 in your Research Companion. Use your investigative skills to look for information that tells you what is important about being an American citizen. Then summarize these points in the space below.

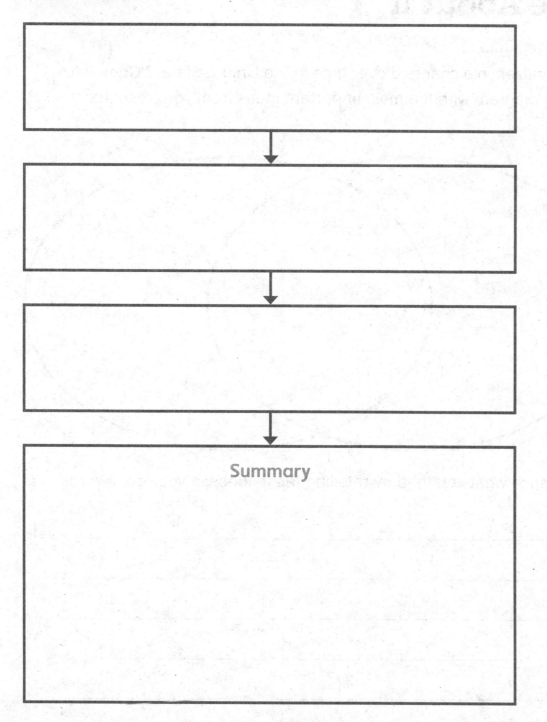

Summary

Think About It

Identify Differences

Based on your research, how do you think citizenship in the United States is different today than it was when this country was founded?

Write About It

Write and Cite Evidence

How has citizenship changed over time in the United States? Complete the Venn diagram with the most important ideas from your research.

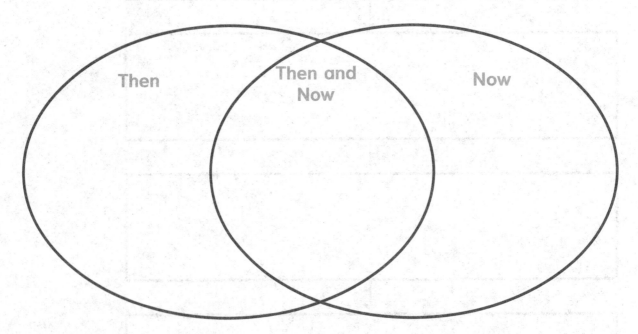

Then

Then and Now

Now

Now summarize what you read by retelling these ideas in your own words.

_____

_____

_____

_____

Talk About It

COLLABORATE

Compare and Contrast

Compare your Venn diagram and summary with a partner. In what ways
are your ideas similar and different?

Connect to the

Civics

Pull It Together

How does being a good citizen benefit your community and the United States?

_____

_____

_____

_____

_____

Inquiry Project Notes

_____

_____

_____

_____

_____

_____

_____

Lesson Outcomes

What Am I Learning?

In this lesson, you will use your investigative skills to learn about real people who helped make their communities and the nation better.

Why Am I Learning It?

Reading and talking about American heroes will help you understand how people have solved problems.

How Will I Know That I Learned It?

You will be able to write about real Americans who helped solve problems in the nation or their communities.

Talk About It

COLLABORATE

Look closely at the picture on the next page. Who is the most important person? Why do you think that?

sharpstock/Alamy Stock Photo

Anne Hutchinson defends her actions during her trial in the colony of Massachusetts.

North Wind Picture Archives/Alamy Stock Photo

1 Inspect

Read the text all the way through.

- **Circle** words you don't know.
- **Underline** clues that tell you who Anne Hutchinson was.
- **Underline** clues that tell you where she lived.
- **Discuss** with a partner why Anne Hutchinson was on trial.

My Notes

_____

_____

_____

_____

_____

_____

_____

_____

_____

_____

Anne Hutchinson: A Hero for Freedom

Anne Hutchinson was born in England. Her father taught her to think for herself and to speak her mind. Anne sailed to Massachusetts with her family in 1634. They settled in Boston.

Anne was very religious. She began to have meetings in her home. At these meetings, she talked about religion. She believed God taught everyone, not just ministers and men. Her ideas were different from what the people in her community taught and believed.

The ministers who disagreed with Anne had her arrested. She was put on trial. During her trial, Anne Hutchinson stood by what she believed. She said only God could be her judge.

The court ordered Anne to leave the community. She left, but she never gave up her ideas or her right to think for herself.

PRIMARY SOURCE

In Their Words...
Anne Hutchinson

"Now, if you do condemn me for speaking what in my conscience I know to be truth I must commit myself unto the Lord."

—The Examination of Mrs. Anne Hutchinson at the Court at Newton, 1637

TEXT: Historical Collections of the Essex Institute Volume III. Salem, MA: G.M. Whipple & A.A. Smith, 1861.

The court orders Anne Hutchinson to leave Boston.

2 Find Evidence

Reread the quote from Anne Hutchinson. How does this show her beliefs?

Underline words and sentences from the text that show how Anne stood up for her beliefs.

3 Make Connections

Talk Discuss with a partner why it is important to stand up for something you believe in.

COLLABORATE

Connect to Now Who is someone today who stands up for what he or she believes?

Explore Cause and Effect

A **cause** is why something happens. An **effect** is what happens. Thinking about causes and effects will help you understand events you read about.

1. **Read the text once all the way through.**
   This will help you understand what the text is about.

2. **Reread the text and look for something that tells you what happened. This is the effect.**

3. **Reread the text again and look for a detail that tells you *why* it happened. This is the cause.**

 COLLABORATE Based on the text you read, work with your class to complete the chart below.

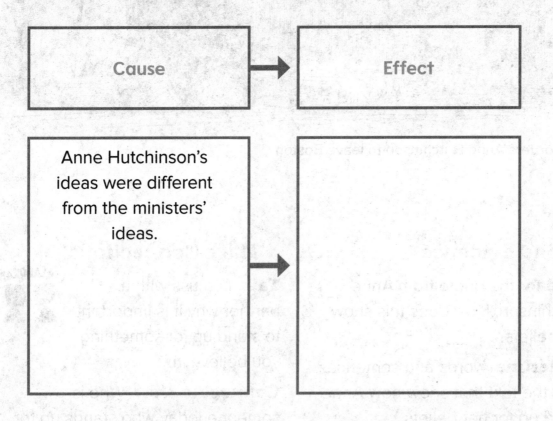

Cause	→	Effect

| Anne Hutchinson's ideas were different from the ministers' ideas. | → | |

Investigate!

Read pages 216–225 in your Research Companion. Use your investigative skills to look for text evidence that tells you what American heroes did and how their actions affected others. This chart will help you organize your notes.

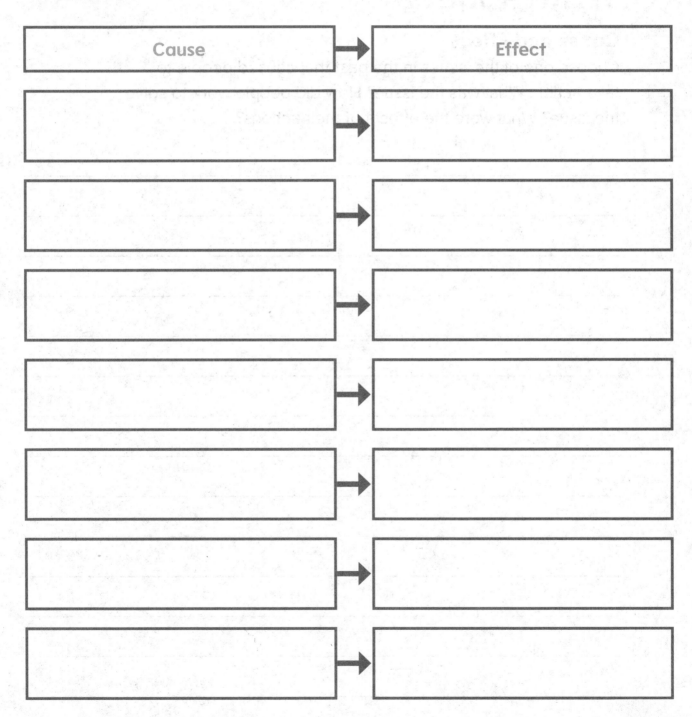

Cause		Effect
	→	
	→	
	→	
	→	
	→	
	→	
	→	

Think About It

Examine

Review your research. What are some problems in the past that Americans have tried to solve?

Write About It

Cause and Effect

Choose one of the issues in the past that caused people to take action. What was the issue? How did people work to solve the issue? What were the effects of their actions?

_____

_____

_____

_____

_____

_____

_____

_____

_____

_____

_____

Talk About It

COLLABORATE

Defend Your Claim

Share your paragraph with a partner. Discuss how the person or people you wrote about helped make the United States a better place.

Connect to the

Civics

ESSENTIAL QUESTION

Pull It Together

In what ways can Americans work together to solve problems in a community?

_____

_____

_____

_____

ESSENTIAL EQ QUESTION

Inquiry Project Notes

_____

_____

_____

_____

_____

_____

Lesson Outcomes

What Am I Learning?

In this lesson, you will use your investigative skills to explore what makes a strong community.

Why Am I Learning It?

Reading and talking about how **citizens** can work together will help you learn more about how people make a difference in their communities.

How Will I Know That I Learned It?

You will be able to describe the characteristics of good leaders. You also will be able to write a paragraph that explains how citizens can help their communities.

COLLABORATE

Talk About It

Read the quote from Dorothy Height. Why do you think she says that it is important not to "go it alone"?

Look closely at the photo on the next page. What are the people doing? How do you think this activity helps the community?

Leland Bobbe/Digital Vision/Getty Images

HSS.3.4.2

PRIMARY SOURCE

In Their Words... Dorothy Height

"I like to say to young people today, you are the beneficiaries of what a lot of people worked and gave their lives for.... And the important thing now is not to go it alone on your own, by yourself, but see how you will join with others. Get organized in how you will serve others and how you will help to move this forward."

—Civil Rights and Women's Rights Activist, NPR Interview, 2008

Building Community

1 Inspect

Read the text and look at the photo.

- **Circle** words you don't know.
- **Underline** words and phrases that help you understand what a community is.
- **State** in a sentence what this text is about.

My Notes

_____

_____

_____

_____

_____

_____

_____

_____

_____

_____

We are all part of a community. When someone asks where we live, we might say the name of our town or state. We might also say we live in the United States. All three answers are correct.

A community can also be a neighborhood, a school, or even a classroom. A community is made up of very different kinds of people. But the people in a community all share certain beliefs, **rights**, and responsibilities.

Think about the different communities you belong to. What kinds of beliefs, rights, and responsibilities do you share with other people in those communities?

In a strong community, people try to do what is best for everybody. They try to build a community that is good for everyone. This can mean following rules and laws. It can also mean working to help solve problems in the community and volunteering to help make the community a better place for all who live there.

What are some ways you can help make your community better?

Volunteers help to keep their community's beach clean.

2 Find Evidence

Reread How does the author say we can build stronger communities?

Underline clues that support what you think.

3 Make Connections

Talk Discuss with a partner what is happening in the photo. How is this an example of community service? Talk about other ways people can volunteer to serve their communities. If you had an opportunity to volunteer in your community, what would you like to do?

COLLABORATE

Explore Drawing Conclusions

A **conclusion** is a decision you make about a topic. You use what you already know and information from what you are reading to draw a conclusion. We draw conclusions when we read. We also draw conclusions from information we see in a map, chart, graph, or photo.

1. **Read the title of the selection or the caption on an image.**
   This will help you understand what the text or image is about.

2. **Read the text all the way through or look closely at the image.**

3. **Think about what you read or saw.**
   Think about the topic. What information did you find in the text or image about the topic? What did you already know?

4. **Draw a conclusion.**
   Use information from the text and image with what you already know to draw a conclusion about the topic.

COLLABORATE Based on the text and photo, work with your class to draw a conclusion about what makes a strong community. Then work with your class to complete the chart below.

What Makes a Strong Community	
Text Clues and What I Already Know	Conclusions

Investigate!

Read pages 226–233 in your Research Companion. Use your investigative skills to look for text evidence that tells you how citizens can build strong communities. This chart will help you organize your notes.

Text Clues and What I Already Know	Conclusions
California leaders who made a difference:	How to build a strong community:
Characteristics of good leaders:	
Problems in my community:	
Ways to make a difference in my community:	

Think About It

Identify

Review your research and the problems discussed in the lesson.
Think about a problem that affects your community right now.

Write About It

Explain

Write a paragraph describing a problem that exists in your
community today. How would you solve the problem?

_____

_____

_____

_____

_____

_____

_____

_____

_____

_____

_____

Talk About It

Discuss and Compare

Share your paragraph with a partner. Compare your problems and solutions. Ask for a different solution to the problem you wrote about. Offer a different solution for your partner's problem.

Civics

Connect to the

Take Action

How can people in a community work together to make it a better place?

_____

_____

_____

_____

 Inquiry Project Notes

_____

_____

_____

_____

_____

_____

Inquiry Project Wrap-Up

Creating a Classroom Constitution

Now is the time for your class to sign and post your classroom constitution. Here's what to do.

☐ Read the constitution aloud.

☐ Review the rules and the consequences for breaking them.

☐ Explain how these were chosen and discuss their purpose.

☐ Sign the constitution and promise to follow it.

☐ Post the constitution in your classroom.

Tips for Collaborating

Remember these tips when you work on the class project.

☐ Share your thoughts and ideas clearly.

☐ Listen and add to the ideas of others.

☐ Ask questions to clarify any misunderstandings.

☐ Work together, and have fun!

Project Rubric

Use these questions to help evaluate your project.

	Yes	No
Are the purpose and goals of the classroom constitution clearly stated?		
Did everyone participate in making the rules?		
Did the class have to make any compromises?		
Are the consequences for breaking the rules fair?		
Do you think having a written constitution will help make your classroom a fair and safe place?		

Project Reflection

Think about the work you did on this project, either with a group or on your own. Describe something that you think you did very well. What could you have done to make your individual or group work better?

_____

_____

_____

_____

Chapter 5

Economics of the Local Region

How Do People in a Community Meet Their Needs?

In this chapter, you will learn about the resources businesses use to make our economy strong. You will also explore how businesses make money and why they spend it. With a team, you will work on a chapter project to write a blog about a local business and how it helps your community.

Talk About It

Discuss with a partner the questions you have about how businesses in your area make money.

My Research Questions

1. _____

_____

2. _____

_____

Inquiry Project

Blogging About a Local Business

In this project, you will work with a small group to create a blog about a local business and describe how it helps your community.

Here's your project checklist.

☐ **Select** a local business in your community.

☐ **Create** a list of questions to ask the business owner. Ask about the owner's background, the company's resources and goods or services, and how the business helps the community meet its needs.

☐ **Conduct** an interview with the owner of the business.

☐ **Determine** what information should be included on the blog and how you will present it.

☐ **Write** a blog on the business you selected, using the information you have gathered. Add pictures, charts, or graphs to support your ideas.

☐ **Share** your blog with your class and have them comment on your findings.

Explore Words

Complete this chapter's Word Rater. Write notes as you learn more about each word.

benefit

My Notes

☐ Know It!
☐ Heard It!
☐ Don't Know It!

_____
_____
_____

capital resources

My Notes

☐ Know It!
☐ Heard It!
☐ Don't Know It!

_____
_____
_____

economy

My Notes

☐ Know It!
☐ Heard It!
☐ Don't Know It!

_____
_____
_____

export

My Notes

☐ Know It!
☐ Heard It!
☐ Don't Know It!

_____
_____
_____

human capital

My Notes

☐ Know It!
☐ Heard It!
☐ Don't Know It!

_____
_____
_____

human resources

My Notes

☐ Know It!

☐ Heard It!

☐ Don't Know It!

_____

_____

_____

import

My Notes

☐ Know It!

☐ Heard It!

☐ Don't Know It!

_____

_____

_____

income

My Notes

☐ Know It!

☐ Heard It!

☐ Don't Know It!

_____

_____

_____

manufacture

My Notes

☐ Know It!

☐ Heard It!

☐ Don't Know It!

_____

_____

_____

profit

My Notes

☐ Know It!

☐ Heard It!

☐ Don't Know It!

_____

_____

_____

How Do Businesses Use Resources?

Lesson Outcomes

What Am I Learning?

In this lesson, you will use your investigative skills to find out what kinds of resources businesses use.

Why Am I Learning It?

Reading and talking about resources will help you understand how businesses in California provide goods and services.

How Will I Know That I Learned It?

You will be able to describe a business in California that is affected by the environment.

Talk About It

COLLABORATE

Look closely at the photographs. In which region do you think each industry takes place? How do you know?

HSS.3.5.1, HSS.3.5.2

Each of California's geographic regions has important industries.

Read the title. What do you think this text will be about?

- **Circle** the fruits and nuts produced in California.
- **Underline** clues in the text that tell you why the Central Valley region is good for agriculture.

My Notes

_____

_____

_____

_____

_____

_____

_____

_____

_____

Agriculture in the Central Valley

Agriculture is a major industry in California. Two-thirds of the country's fruits and nuts come from California. Grapes, strawberries, tomatoes, almonds, and walnuts are some of the top crops produced in the state.

The majority of these fruits and nuts are grown in the Central Valley region. This region is ideal for agriculture because of its fertile land and mild climate. There are two rivers that run through the region that provide water for the crops.

Many farms are located in the Central Valley. These businesses depend on the land to be successful. They sell the crops they harvest in order to make money. Some crops, such as almonds, are sold all over the world.

Exactostock/SuperStock

Harvesting tomatoes in California

2 Find Evidence

Reread the text. How do farmers depend on the land to be successful?

Examine the second sentence in the second paragraph. What does the word *ideal* mean?

3 Make Connections

Talk with a partner about how the environment affects farming businesses in the Central Valley.

COLLABORATE

Explore Main Idea and Details

The main idea is what the text is about. Details tell you more about the main idea.

1. **Read the text all the way through.**
   This will help you understand what the text is about.

2. **Reread the text and look for the most important point.**
   The most important point is the main idea. Look for a sentence that states the main idea.

3. **Look for ideas that tell you more about the most important point.**
   These ideas are the details.

 COLLABORATE Based on the text you read, work with your class to complete the chart.

Main Idea	Details
Agriculture is a major industry in California.	

Investigate!

Read pages 240–247 in your Research Companion. Use your investigative skills to look for text evidence that tells you how businesses use resources. This chart will help you organize your notes.

Main Idea	Details

Think About It

Examine

Based on your research, what types of businesses are found in California?

Write About It

Describe

Write a paragraph describing a business that you think is affected by the environment. Give reasons to support your answer.

_____

_____

_____

_____

_____

_____

_____

_____

_____

_____

_____

_____

_____

Talk About It

COLLABORATE

Give Reasons

Talk to a classmate who chose a different business. Take turns discussing your opinion and reasons why you chose that business. Do you agree or disagree with your partner's opinion?

Connect to the EQ

Economics

Summarize

How do businesses in your community use resources to help people meet their needs?

_____

_____

_____

 Inquiry Project Notes

_____

_____

_____

_____

_____

_____

Lesson 2

How Have Goods and Services Changed Over Time?

Lesson Outcomes

What Am I Learning?

In this lesson, you will use your investigative skills to learn how goods and services in California have changed over time.

Why Am I Learning It?

Reading and talking about these changes will help you understand how California's communities use goods and services.

How Will I Know That I Learned It?

You will be able to write and talk about the goods and services you would have used in your community 100 years ago.

Talk About It

COLLABORATE

Look closely at the photo on the next page. Are these people buying goods or services? Who provides them?

Exactostock/SuperStock

TRAIN, GIANT SLIDE, MINI SLIDE, PLAY
RIDE, PUMPKIN JUMP, FERRIS WHEEL, HELICOPTER RIDE

ALL TICKETS VALID THRU OCT. 31
NO CASH REFUNDS ON TICKETS WILL BE GIVEN

PUMPKIN STATION PACK $24.00
INCLUDES ONE TICKET FOR EVERY RIDE   (11 TICKETS)
INCLUDING THE PETTING ZOO

___UE PACK $42.00
___ TICKETS FOR EVERY RIDE   (22 TICKETS)
___TTING ZOO

___CK $56.00
___CKET   (33 TICKETS)
___ THE PETTING ZOO

___E PACK $22.00
___ ONE TICKET FOR EVERY RIDE   (10 TICKETS)
___ OR THE PETTING ZOO

___INDIVIDUAL TICKET PRICES
___.75 PER RIDE, AND PETTING ZOO

Buying tickets for rides
at an amusement park

1 Inspect

Read the title. What do you think this text will be about?

- **Circle** words that you don't know.
- **Underline** clues that tell you:
  - What shopping was like long ago
  - What shopping is like today
- **Discuss** with a partner how shopping in California has changed over time.

My Notes

_____

_____

_____

_____

_____

_____

_____

_____

_____

Long ago, most towns had only a few small stores, and each store carried only a few different items. There might have been one kind of soap or one kind of cereal. Most of the items were made nearby. Items that came from far away were expensive and not easy to get. It was hard to bring a special item from another country to a small store in California.

Customers who walked to a store could buy only a few items at a time. If they rode in a wagon, they could bring home more items.

Shopping at a small store long ago

At a mall, people can shop at many different stores that sell a variety of goods.

2 Find Evidence

Reread the text. How do these changes in how people shop affect the local economy?

Draw a box around clues.

3 Make Connections

Talk about why people shop at a mall. What goods or services do they need? COLLABORATE

Today, people often shop at large stores or malls. There, they can find goods from around the world at low prices. There is also a lot of variety. People can buy many different kinds of soap. The same items are available all year long. People also have many ways to pay for these items. They can use cash, credit cards, smartphones, or checks.

Customers often drive to the store. This makes it easier to bring home many things at one time.

Sometimes, shoppers still prefer small stores. They like knowing that the goods are made right in the community. These customers are willing to pay more for a special handmade item at a local store.

Andrew Resek/McGraw-Hill Education

Explore Compare and Contrast

To **compare** means to see how things are alike. To **contrast** means to see how they are different. Your social studies text sometimes will compare and contrast life in the past with life in the present.

1. **Read the text all the way through.**
   This will help you understand what the text is about.

2. **Reread the text. Look for things that have stayed the same.**
   This will tell you how the past and present are alike.

3. **Then look for details that tell you what has changed.**
   This will tell you how the past and present are different.

COLLABORATE Based on the text you read, work with your class to complete the chart.

Shopping

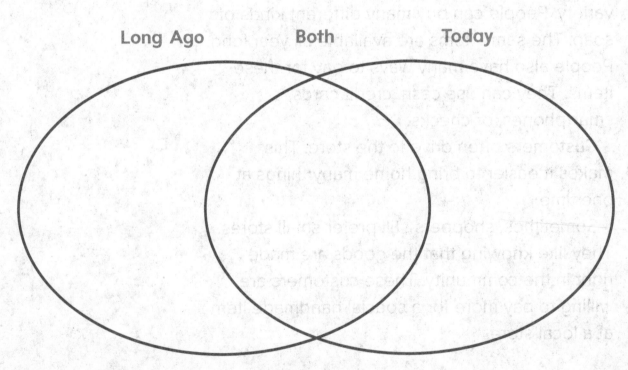
Long Ago   Both   Today

Investigate!

Read pages 248–253 in your Research Companion. Use your investigative skills to look for text evidence that tells you how goods and services have changed over time. This chart will help you organize your notes.

Goods and Services

Long Ago   Both   Today

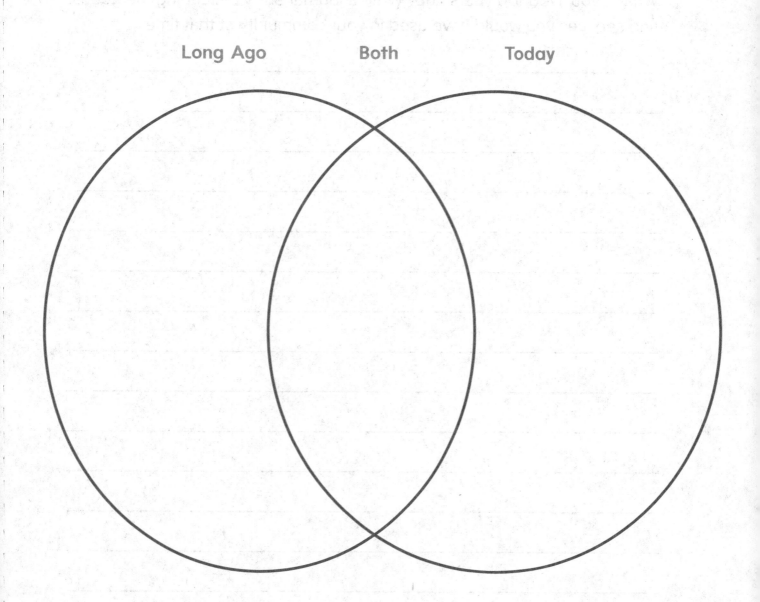

Think About It

Examine

Based on your research, what goods and services have businesses in California provided?

Write About It

Imagine

What if you lived 100 years ago? Write a journal entry describing the goods and services you would have used in your community at that time.

_____

_____

_____

_____

_____

_____

_____

_____

_____

_____

_____

Talk About It

COLLABORATE

Discuss

Share your journal entry with a partner. Discuss how the goods and services in your community have changed over time.

Economics

Connect to the

ESSENTIAL EQ QUESTION

Look at Our Community

What goods and services do businesses in your community provide? How do these goods and services help people meet their needs?

_____

_____

_____

_____

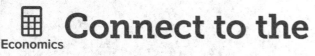

ESSENTIAL EQ QUESTION

Inquiry Project Notes

_____

_____

_____

_____

_____

_____

Lesson Outcomes

What Am I Learning?
In this lesson, you will use your investigative skills to find out how businesses make money.

Why Am I Learning It?
Reading and talking about how businesses make money will help you understand how people make money around the world.

How Will I Know That I Learned It?
You will be able to write a paragraph explaining how businesses make a **profit** by selling goods and services.

Talk About It

COLLABORATE

Look closely at the photo. What are these people doing? What kind of business is this? How can you tell?

netsuthep summat/123RF

Workers in a business sell goods and services.

The American Dream

Many people want the "American Dream." They want to have the chance to succeed—to get a good job, own a home, or run their own business.

The **economy** of the United States is based on the success of its citizens. People must have jobs and earn money in a successful economy. Businesses create jobs. They hire people to make and sell their goods and services.

PRIMARY SOURCE

In Their Words... Thomas Perez

"Our workforce and our entire economy are strongest when we embrace diversity to its fullest, and that means opening doors of opportunity to everyone and recognizing that the American Dream excludes no one."

—Thomas Perez, U.S. Secretary of Labor (2013–2017)

All the workers in a business help the business succeed.

Workers are important to any business. A business cannot operate without people doing their jobs. A good business will have many different kinds of workers. They may have different skills. Some workers will make the goods. Others will provide a service. When people work together, it makes the business a better place to work. The work they do allows the business to earn money. In this way both the workers and the business are successful. Success gives people the opportunity to improve their lives.

2 Find Evidence

Reread the quote. What does former Secretary of Labor Thomas Perez think makes our economy strong?

Examine What do you think Mr. Perez means by the phrase "the American Dream excludes no one"?

3 Make Connections

Talk Discuss with a partner why a business needs workers to be successful.

COLLABORATE

Explore Making Inferences

When you read, you often make inferences about the text. An **inference** is a decision you make about the meaning of the text. To make an inference:

1. **Read the text once all the way through.**
   This will help you understand what the text is about.

2. **Think about what you read.**
   An author may not always tell you everything. What questions do you have?

3. **Think about what you already know about this topic.**

4. **Make a decision about the text.**
   Base your decision on what you know and what you read.

COLLABORATE Based on the text you read, work with your class to complete the chart.

Text Clues and What I Already Know	Inferences
Thomas Perez says we should recognize that "the American Dream excludes no one." I know:	Mr. Perez means that:

Investigate!

Read pages 254–263 in your Research Companion. Use your investigative skills to make inferences about how businesses in the United States make money. This chart will help you organize your notes.

Text Clues and What I Already Know	Inferences
Goods are moved around the world in many ways. Airplanes move some goods. But most goods are moved to and from the United States on cargo ships. I know:	This quote means:
The infographic showing where T-shirts are made. I know:	This diagram means:
Some women in the Middle East have created online businesses. They can earn money while they care for their families at home. I know:	This text means:

Think About It

Examine
Based on your research, how do you think businesses are able to make money?

Write About It

State the Main idea
Why do businesses manufacture goods and provide services?

_____

_____

_____

Write and Cite Evidence
How do businesses make a profit? Use facts from the text to explain your response.

_____

_____

_____

_____

_____

_____

_____

_____

Talk About It

Explain

With a partner, discuss how making a profit can help a business continue to meet people's needs.

 # Connect to the

Economics

Look at Our Community

How can successful businesses help the people in your community succeed?

_____

_____

_____

_____

_____

_____

 Inquiry Project Notes

_____

_____

_____

_____

_____

4

How Can People Spend Money Wisely?

Lesson Outcomes

What Am I Learning?
In this lesson, you will use your investigative skills to explore how people choose to spend money.

Why Am I Learning It?
Reading and talking about how people make spending choices will help you make good choices about spending your money.

How Will I Know That I Learned It?
You will be able to write a list of questions that you should ask yourself before you spend money.

COLLABORATE
Talk About It

Look closely at the picture on the next page. What do you think the children are discussing? What choices do they have to make? How will they decide?

D. Hurst/Alamy Stock Photo

Thinking before you buy helps you make good spending choices.

1 Inspect

Read the title. What do you think this text will be about?

- **Underline** questions you should ask before buying something.

My Notes

_____

_____

_____

_____

_____

_____

_____

_____

_____

_____

_____

_____

_____

Good Money Choices

What would you spend money on? Would you buy something you need or something you want? Would you take time to think about your purchase before making it? It is important to ask yourself some questions before you buy something. You might ask: Is this something I really need? Is the most expensive item the best choice? Will a less expensive item be just as good? Can I do without it? Do I have enough money? Should I save my money for something else I really need or want?

> **PRIMARY SOURCE**

In Their Words... Benjamin Franklin

"Beware of little expenses, a small leak will sink a great ship."

—*Poor Richard's Almanack*

People spend money on things that they need and on things that they want.

It takes time to earn money. So, people need to make good choices when they spend money.
People buy things they need, such as food. They buy other things because they want them. People need to think about the costs and **benefits** of buying an item. It's easy to spend money without thinking about it. But that could mean they may not have enough to buy something they really need later.

2 Find Evidence

Reread What is the difference between a want and a need?

Examine the text. What examples does it give of wants and needs?

3 Make Connections

Talk With a partner, discuss Benjamin Franklin's statement. What does it mean? Do you agree? Why or why not?

COLLABORATE

Dirk Lindner/Image Source

Explore Main Ideas and Details

The **main idea** is the most important idea of a paragraph, a section, or an article. **Details** tell more about the main idea. When you read, it is helpful to focus on the main ideas.

1. **Read the text all the way through.**
   This will help you understand what the text is about.

2. **Think about what you read.**
   Ask yourself: *What is it about? What is the author trying to say?*

3. **In each section of the text, look for a main idea.**
   Section titles will give you clues. Sometimes the first or last paragraph in a section contains the main idea.

4. **Look for key details that tell more about the main ideas.**

 COLLABORATE Based on the text you read, work with your class to complete the chart.

	Main Idea	Details
Good Money Choices		

Investigate!

Read pages 264–271 in your Research Companion. Use your investigative skills to look for text evidence that tells you the main ideas and their supporting details. This chart will help you organize your notes.

	Main Idea	Details
Using Money		
Earning Money to Help Others		
Making Economic Choices		
Building Your Own Capital		

Think About It

Examine

Based on your research, what will help you make good choices about spending money?

Write About It

Define

What is a want? What is a need?

_____

_____

_____

_____

Write and Cite Evidence

What questions should you consider before you buy something? Use details from the text to explain your response.

_____

_____

_____

_____

_____

_____

Talk About It

COLLABORATE

Discuss

Compare your list with a partner. Discuss why these questions are important. Which questions do you and your partner think are most important?

Economics

Connect to the

Look at Our Community

How does making good money choices help people in your community meet their needs?

_____

_____

_____

_____

_____

Inquiry Project Notes

_____

_____

_____

_____

_____

Studying the
Stars

CHARACTERS

Narrator

Dad

Mom

Ava

Theo
(Ava's younger brother)

Beth
(Ava's friend)

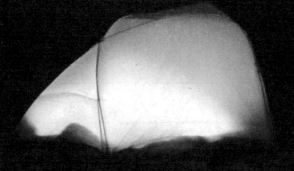

VCNW/iStock/Getty Images

Narrator: Ava's family is camping for the weekend. They are up in the mountains. Without city lights, it is easier to see what's in the night sky. Ava's Dad shows her a group of stars that form a shape in the sky.

Dad: *(pointing to the sky)* There's the Big Dipper. Can you see it?

Ava: I think so. It looks like a scoop.

Mom: Yes. Look at the two stars on the outer edge of the dipper. You can use those two stars to find the North Star.

Ava: I think I see it. Is it that bright one?

Dad: Yes, that's it.

Theo: I'm not sure I see it.

Ava: *(pointing to help her brother)* Look over there. It's brighter than the other stars.

Dad: The North Star is also called Polaris.

Ava: Wow! There are so many stars. I wonder what else is out there.

Theo: Aliens!

(Ava at home with her family)

Narrator: Ava is excited about looking at the stars. At school, Ava learns about astronomy. She finds out that she can look at stars through a telescope. Ava has an idea. She tells her family about it at dinner.

Ava: I've been thinking about how much I like looking at the stars. I'm going to need a telescope.

Dad: A telescope? Really? Is that something you need or just something you want?

Ava: I guess it's just something I want. But if I'm going to be an astronomer, I want to start studying the stars right now.

Theo: What's an astronomer?

Mom: Someone who studies the stars and planets in the universe.

Ava: That's right. That's what I want to do.

Dad: That's great, but do you know what a telescope costs?

Ava: Not really.

Dad: Then you need to find out. Our budget right now doesn't include buying a telescope. You might need to save up some money if you want one.

Theo: What's a budget?

Mom: It's a plan for how we spend our income.

Theo: What's an income?

Mom: It's the money we receive for working.

Ava: Hmmm. I need a plan.

Narrator: After dinner, Ava searches the Internet. She finds out that a new telescope can cost a lot of money. Much more than she expected. Then she asks Mom for help.

Ava: I found out how much telescopes cost, and I need a plan.

Mom: Is a telescope that important to you?

Ava: Yes. I want to study the stars. Maybe I'll make an important discovery someday.

Mom: Is it more important than the new game you wanted to buy?

Ava: Yes, I think so.

Mom: Well . . . you can always save the money you get for your birthday.

Ava: Good idea, but I'll need more.

Mom: How about doing some extra chores around the house? We could probably pay you a little.

Ava: Really? That would be great! What can I do?

Mom: Let's make a list of jobs you could do.

Ava: OK. I'll get my tablet.

Mom: Let's see, in addition to your normal chores, you can help me walk Max.

Ava: OK. How about the recycling? I could take care of that every week.

Mom: That sounds good. And Theo could use your help to learn his spelling words.

Ava: I guess I could do that.

Mom: There are some jobs that we only need help with at certain times— like raking leaves and pulling weeds.

Ava: I'll put those on the list.

(A few days later, at Ava's home)

Narrator: Ava comes home from walking Max, the family dog. Her friend Beth is waiting for her.

Beth: Wow, you've been busy!

Ava: Yes, I walk Max every day—with my mom— but it's my job to clean up after him.

Beth: Yuk!

Ava: My mom and I made a list of jobs I can do. It keeps me busy.

Beth: How much money have you saved for your telescope?

Ava: Well, not much yet. It will take a while to save what I need.

Beth: How long?

Ava: I'm not sure, but I think it will be several months. I already have some birthday money saved that I can use.

Beth: You must really want a telescope!

Ava: I do! It's worth giving up some of my time to earn extra money. I can't wait to go camping again and look at the stars through a telescope!

Beth: Can I come?

Ava: Sure!

Talk About It

COLLABORATE

Talk Tell a partner about something you really wanted. What did you give up to get it? What were the benefits of getting the item?

Inquiry Project Wrap-Up

Blogging About a Local Business

Now is the time for your team to share your blog with the class. Then as a class you will discuss the different businesses that make up your community. Here's what to do.

☐ Present your blog to the class.

☐ Describe how this business helps your community meet its needs.

☐ Review and respond to the comments that classmates wrote on your blog.

☐ Discuss as a class the different types of businesses that are part of your community.

Tips for Presenting

Remember these tips when you present to your class.

☐ Make sure everyone can see you and your presentation.

☐ Speak loudly, clearly, and not too fast.

☐ Listen to your audience and respect their opinions.

☐ Relax and enjoy yourself!

Project Rubric

Use these questions to help evaluate your project.

	Yes	No
Was your team well prepared for the interview?		
Did you have to follow up with the business owner to get more information?		
Was the information in your blog written well and without errors?		
Did you provide any images, charts, or graphs in your blog?		
Did your blog's structure make sense to your readers?		
Did all your team members do their fair share of the work?		

Project Reflection

Think about the work you did on this project. Describe something that you think you or your team did well. What might you do in the future to improve your work?

_____

_____

_____

Reference Section

The Reference Section has a glossary of vocabulary words from the chapters in this book. Use this section to explore new vocabulary as you investigate and take action.

Glossary

A

amendment a change to a document

aqueduct a manmade channel used to transport water

B

benefit something that helps a person

C

capital resources goods such as tools and machines that businesses use to provide goods or services

century one hundred years

citizen a person who lives in a community or is a member of a country

climate the weather a place has over a long period of time

community place where people live, work, and play

compromise an agreement that people make when they have different ideas

conserve to use something, such as water, without wasting it

constitution a written plan of government

culture the way of life a group of people share

D

decade ten years

drought a shortage of water due to lack of rainfall

economy the production, buying, and selling of goods and services

elevation how high an area of land is above sea level

entrepreneur a person who starts and runs his or her own business

environment the surroundings or conditions in which someone lives

ethnic group a group of people who share the same culture

executive branch the part of government that makes sure that laws are carried out and followed

expedition a journey, especially by a group of people, for a specific purpose

explorer a person who travels to learn more about other places

export to send goods to another country for sale; an item transported to another country for sale there

federal national

harvest to gather in a crop; the crop that has been gathered in

human capital the skills and knowledge a person has to do a job

human resources people in a business who provide valuable skills

import to bring goods into a country from another country to sell; an item brought into a country for sale there

income money earned by working

industry a group of businesses that provides a specific product or service

innovation a new idea, piece of equipment, or method

judicial branch the part of government that decides what the laws mean

jury a group of citizens who are chosen to decide a legal case

legislative branch the part of government that makes the laws

manufacture to make products using machinery

migrate to move to a new area

mission a church or a settlement built around a church

N

natural resource something found in nature that people use

nomad a person who moves from place to place

P

pollution anything that makes the air, water, or soil dirty

population the number of people who live in one place

precipitation water that falls to the ground as rain, snow, sleet, or hail

profit money gained after operating expenses are subtracted

R

region an area of land with certain features that make it different from other areas

reservation land set aside for American Indians

right something that is due to everyone

S

settlers people who move to a new country or area in order to live there

T

tax money collected by a government

traditions beliefs or customs handed down from the past, such as from parents to children

V

vegetation plants found in a specific area

Grade Three

Historical and Social Sciences Content Standards and Analysis Skills

History-Social Sciences Content Standards

Continuity and Change

Students in grade three learn more about our connections to the past and the ways in which particularly local, but also regional and national, government and traditions have developed and left their marks on current society, providing common memories. Emphasis is on the physical and cultural landscape of California, including the study of American Indians, the subsequent arrival of immigrants, and the impact they have had in forming the character of our contemporary society.

3.1 Students describe the physical and human geography and use maps, tables, graphs, photographs, and charts to organize information about people, places, and environments in a spatial context.

1. Identify geographical features in their local region (e.g., deserts, mountains, valleys, hills, coastal areas, oceans, lakes).

2. Trace the ways in which people have used the resources of the local region and modified the physical environment (e.g., a dam constructed upstream changed a river or coastline).

3.2 Students describe the American Indian nations in their local region long ago and in the recent past.

1. Describe national identities, religious beliefs, customs, and various folklore traditions.

2. Discuss the ways in which physical geography, including climate, influenced how the local Indian nations adapted to their natural environment (e.g., how they obtained food, clothing, tools).

3. Describe the economy and systems of government, particularly those with tribal constitutions, and their relationship to federal and state governments.

4. Discuss the interaction of new settlers with the already established Indians of the region.

3.3 Students draw from historical and community resources to organize the sequence of local historical events and describe how each period of settlement left its mark on the land.

1. Research the explorers who visited here, the newcomers who settled here, and the people who continue to come to the region, including their cultural and religious traditions and contributions.

2. Describe the economies established by settlers and their influence on the present-day economy, with emphasis on the importance of private property and entrepreneurship.

3. Trace why their community was established, how individuals and families contributed to its founding and development, and how the community has changed over time, drawing on maps, photographs, oral histories, letters, newspapers, and other primary sources.

3.4 Students understand the role of rules and laws in our daily lives and the basic structure of the U.S. government.

1. Determine the reasons for rules, laws, and the U.S. Constitution; the role of citizenship in the promotion of rules and laws; and the consequences for people who violate rules and laws.

2. Discuss the importance of public virtue and the role of citizens, including how to participate in a classroom, in the community, and in civic life.

3. Know the histories of important local and national landmarks, symbols, and essential documents that create a sense of community among citizens and exemplify cherished ideals (e.g., the U.S. flag, the bald eagle, the Statue of Liberty, the U.S. Constitution, the Declaration of Independence, the U.S. Capitol).

4. Understand the three branches of government, with an emphasis on local government.

5. Describe the ways in which California, the other states, and sovereign American Indian tribes contribute to the making of our nation and participate in the federal system of government.

6. Describe the lives of American heroes who took risks to secure our freedoms (e.g., Anne Hutchinson, Benjamin Franklin, Thomas Jefferson, Abraham Lincoln, Frederick Douglass, Harriet Tubman, Martin Luther King, Jr.).

3.5 Students demonstrate basic economic reasoning skills and an understanding of the economy of the local region.

1. Describe the ways in which local producers have used and are using natural resources, human resources, and capital resources to produce goods and services in the past and the present.

2. Understand that some goods are made locally, some elsewhere in the United States, and some abroad.

3. Understand that individual economic choices involve trade-offs and the evaluation of benefits and costs.

4. Discuss the relationship of students' "work" in school and their personal human capital.

Historical and Social Sciences Analysis Skills

In addition to the standards, students demonstrate the following intellectual, reasoning, reflection, and research skills:

Chronological and Spatial Thinking

1. Students place key events and people of the historical era they are studying in a chronological sequence and within a spatial context; they interpret time lines.

2. Students correctly apply terms related to time, including past, present, future, decade, century, and generation.

3. Students explain how the present is connected to the past, identifying both similarities and differences between the two, and how some things change over time and some things stay the same.

4. Students use map and globe skills to determine the absolute locations of places and interpret information available through a map's or globe's legend, scale, and symbolic representations.

5. Students judge the significance of the relative location of a place (e.g., proximity to a harbor, on trade routes) and analyze how relative advantages or disadvantages can change over time.

Research, Evidence, and Point of View

1. Students differentiate between primary and secondary sources.

2. Students pose relevant questions about events they encounter in historical documents, eyewitness accounts, oral histories, letters, diaries, artifacts, photographs, maps, artworks, and architecture.

3. Students distinguish fact from fiction by comparing documentary sources on historical figures and events with fictionalized characters and events.

Historical Interpretation

1. Students summarize the key events of the era they are studying and explain the historical contexts of those events.

2. Students identify the human and physical characteristics of the places they are studying and explain how those features form the unique character of those places.

3. Students identify and interpret the multiple causes and effects of historical events.

4. Students conduct cost-benefit analyses of historical and current events.